SOUTH INDIAN PORTRAITS
in Stone and Metal

By T. G. ARAVAMUTHAN

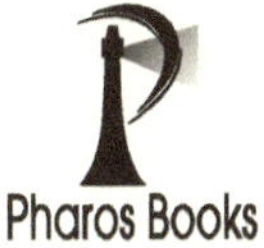

Pharos Books

ISBN: 978-93-90697-49-6
eISBN: 978-93-90697-50-2

©Publisher

Publisher: Pharos Books (P) Ltd.
Plot No.-55, Main Mother Dairy Road
Pandav Nagar, East Delhi-110092
Phone: 011-40395855, +4049916623
WhatsApp: +91 8368220032
E-mail: sales@pharosbooks.in
Website: www.pharosbooks.in
First Edition: 2022

Printed By: Sushma Book Binding House, Okhla
Industrial Area, Phase II, New Delhi-110020

South Indian Portraits in Stone and Metal
By T. G. Aravamuthan

CONTENTS

ACKNOWLEDGEMENTS

For kind permission to utilise a number of photographs, I am indebted to Sir John Marshall, formerly Director-General of Archaeology in India, to Dr. F.H. Gravely, Superintendent of the Government Museum, Madras, to Dr. R. Shama-Sastri, formerly Director of Archaeological Researches, Mysore, and to Prof. H. Heras, St Xavier's College, Bombay.

PREFACE

Becoming interested in the subject of this book in 1921, I pursued my inquiries for some years, and about the middle of 1925, I wrote a short book embodying the results of my studies. A well-known journal devoted to Art undertook to publish the work in its pages, but in 1927 it abandoned the project all of a sudden, though the matter had been in type for months. In December 1927, my friend Mr. K. Ramakotisvara Rao started publishing the work in instalments in his excellent journal, the *Triveni*. When three instalments had appeared, the India Society, London, kindly agreed in April 1928 to bring the work out as one of its publications, and, thereupon the publication of the work in the *Triveni* was stopped. Later, the India Society decided to publish only the earlier chapters of the work: those chapters are now in the press and will be shortly published under the title, *Portrait Sculpture in South India*. The later chapters have gone into the present book, and as they form the sequel to the earlier chapters, this book is the complement to the book which is being published by the India Society. With the view, however, of ensuring a complete presentation of the subject in the present book, I wrote two brief chapters for it,— Chapters I and V,—into which I compressed the data which are set out in full detail in the other book: the summary is bald and meagre, but in fairness to the India Society, I could not make it fuller. The book thus evolved was published serially between June and August of this year in the *Hindu Illustrated Weekly*, Madras, and I am now republishing it in this form with the kind permission of the proprietors of that journal. I have slightly recast the matter in some places, but I am afraid I might have succeeded only in adding obscurity to obscurity.

No pains have been spared to make this book as distinct as may be from the India Society's publication in respect of both the letter-press and the illustrations, and I trust that each would serve as a complement to the other. Perhaps I may add that with a view to avoid repetition of references I have not given in this book such references as have been given in the other.

Though manuscripts of these two books, in their many forms and at various stages, have been in circulation among scholars since 1925, only one attempt to utilise and yet forestall my work has come to my notice: the production being ineffective even as a summary of my work, I have ignored it altogether.

My thanks are due in full measure to a kind friend who has drawn specially for this book the line-sketches used as illustrations. He prefers to remain anonymous and I greatly regret that I am unable to mention his name. Photographic fidelity has not been aimed at in the sketches, but they possess the all too rare quality of suggestiveness. The exposition of the theme of this book has proceeded on lines which have made it impossible for the illustrations to be inserted in juxtaposition with the references to them in the letter-press: I regret the divorce between text and illustration but I am not able to mend it.

I am under deep obligation to my friend, Mr. V. Narayanan, M.A., M.L., Advocate, Madras, for kindly discussing the subject with me in some of its aspects.

I must confess that the conclusions presented in this book must necessarily be tentative till the various *sastras*, inclusive of the *silpa*, the *agama* and the *tantra*,—and the diverse beliefs, practices and customs of the people have been studied with some approach to thoroughness. An humble attempt in that direction will be found in a work, ***The Evolution of the Temple***, which I hope to complete shortly.

LANDON'S GARDENS, KILPAUK,
MADRAS, AUGUST 18, 1980
T. G. ARAVAMUTHAN.

I

A PERSISTENT ART

That portraiture is an art which the Hindus did not cultivate, and had even an aversion to, has been the conviction of some competent authorities on Indian art, but like many other generalizations about Indian culture, that conviction is based on an imperfect acquaintance with facts and on impressions formed when very little was known of things, Indian. Portrait-sculptures have been discovered in almost every part of India, and we can now point to specimens' representative of the work of almost every period in the history of Indian sculpture.[1]

Portrait statuettes are said to have been found in the ruins excavated at Mohenjodaro. Four statues, (two discovered near Patna and two near Mathura), have been claimed to represent four kings of the Sisunaga dynasty, namely, Kunika-Ajatashatru, Udayin-Aja, Darshak and Nandivardhana, who belonged to the 5th century B.C. The earliest sculptures which were indisputably portraits were carved on the walls of a cave in the pass of Nanaghat: they were only reliefs

---

1. For a detailed study of the subject-matter of this Chapter and of Chapter V of this book, see my *Portrait Sculpture in South India.*

and were intended to portray a queen of the Satakarni line who, about the 2nd century B.C., performed certain Vedic sacrifices, and a number of her relations who derived merit from those sacrifices. A later potentate of this line, either Gautamiputra Sri Satakarni I or Gautamiputra Sri-Yajna Satakarni II, belonging to the 2nd century A.D., seems to have been portrayed in a statue which must have been placed in the architectural addenda to the *stupa* at Amaravati. Some *alto-relievos* in the *chaityas* at Karle and Kanheri are indubitably portraits of members of this line. A mutilated statue of Kanishka (c. 120 A.D.) has been discovered at Mathura, and three other statues, discovered along with it or a few miles from it, are contended to be portraits of three members of his line—Chastana, Wema Kadphises, and a son of Kanishka. Among the sculptures discovered in the excavations at Sahri-Bahlol, near Peshawar, are a number of fine images with figures of devotees carved at the base: the devotees worship the Buddha or stand devoutly before incense-bearing altars. In the famous caves at Udayagiri and Khandagiri in Orissa, in a *vihara*-cave at Ajanta, and in one of the caves at Aurangabad, we come across sculptures which cannot but be portraits of devotees, whether of high or of low station in life.

In the medieval period too, the art of portraiture does not seem to have fallen into neglect in north India. In Rajputana especially, the art seems to have been practised with considerable success, and many of the temples of Rajputana are said to contain statues of high artistic value. Statues seem occasionally to be placed in *chhatris* or *devagadhs* raised in the royal cemetries at Bikanir and other capitals of the states of Rajputana, and worship is offered to them every day by priests

            South Indian Portraits in Stone and Metal

of the Sakadvipi Brahman, a caste. In the Kamakhya temple at Gauhati in Assam stand statues of two princes of the 16th century A.D. by whom the temple seems to have been built. Statues are numerous in Nepal and are so well designed and executed that it has been doubted if better statues are found anywhere else in the wide world.

In countries such as Tibet, Ceylon and Java which borrowed much of their culture from India we have ample evidence to establish that portraiture was practised steadily, continuously and successfully.

Nowhere in India, however, has the art had so persistent a life as in south India or such a creditable record of achievement, and nowhere else has the art drawn its inspiration more freely from the fondest beliefs and the deepest convictions of the people.

Mention has been made already of the statue of a Gautamiputra Satakarni at Amaravati and of sculptures portraying other members of the Satakarni line at other places which lay within their extensive dominions. Members of the famous Pallava dynasty of south India are found figured at Mahabalipuram,—Simhavishnu, Mahendravarman I and Narasimhavarman I,—kings who reigned from about 575 to 650 A.D. In a rock-cut cave-temple at Trichinopoly we have two inscriptions which say that Mahendravarman I had a statue of himself installed in the temple, perhaps beside the icon of the deity to whom the temple had been constructed. Among the carvings at Mahabalipuram and Kunnandar Koil are some which, in all probability, portray less known members of this dynasty. In a temple at Pattadakal, we have a pair of figures which are probably portraits of the Chalukyan king, Vikramaditya II (733-47 A.D.) and his queen Trailokya Mahadevi. We have statues of two kings and of two queens of the Chola dynasty and we hear of statues of many of its other members. On the wall of a temple, a low relief of Gandaraditya (c. 960 A.D.), a Chola king who was a saint and a poet, shows him engaged in worship. Statues of his queen, Sembiyan Mahadevi were placed in two temples which she built. Parantaka II (the son of the brother of Gandaraditya) and his queen Vanavan Mahadevi were represented in bronze statues set up in memory of them in the great temple of Tanjore. Gandaraditya's sister's son, 'Pichchan of the Sacred Stone Temple,' is pictured in a short effigy on the wall of another temple. Rajaraja I (the son of Parantaka II) and his queen, Loka Mahadevi, were portrayed in bronze statues of them which were placed in the company of the idols of the gods and goddessess which Rajaraja I installed in the Tanjore temple. A statue of another of his queens, Solamadevi is found in the temple at Kalahasti.

A metal statue of Kulottunga III (1178-1216 A.D.), a distant descendant of Rajaraja I, is found in the same temple. Of some of the kings of Mysore we have excellent representations: Vishnuvardhana (1104-41 A.D.) is portrayed in a beautiful bronze and also in a stone statue: Raja-Odayar (1578-1617 A.D.) and Kanthirava-Narasa-Odayar (1638-59 A.D.) are each figured in two statues: we know of a statue of Dodda-deva-raja-Odayar (1659-72 A.D.). Among sculptural effigies of minor celebrities of the Mysore country, may be mentioned those of a chief of Ummattur, of Bayirappa the Avati chieftain, and of the three brothers, Kempe Gauda, Kempe Somanna and Uligam Basavayya, of the Yala-hanka chieftaincy. At Tirumalai

  South Indian Portraits in Stone and Metal

(Tirupati) we have a fine group of kings of the Vijayanagara dynasty: the statues of Krishnadevaraya (1509-39 A.D.) and his two queens are of copper, in repousse work, and are excelled only by the companion statue of Venkata-raya I (1586-1614 A.D.): Tirumala-raya (1569-72 A.D.) and his queen stand close by, sculptured in stone. Statues of Krishnadevaraya were also set up at Chidambaram and Srisailam. At Madura we have a Hall in which statues of five generations of the Nayaka kings (1529-1652 A.D.) of that place are ranged in the order of succession: though carved to a scale greater than life, the statues do not appear to deviate from the norm, forming, as they do, integral parts of the great pillars which impart an air of grandeur to the Valhalla. Similar galleries of statues are to be found in other temples: a few of the Tanjore Nayakas are figured at Pattisvaram: some Nayakas of Trichinopoly are sculptured in the gallery at Srirangam: representations of chieftains are found carved in the pillared naves of temples at Srimushnam and Nanguneri: some 'Viceroys' are carved to the life in the great Tinnevelly temple: many of the Setupatis are represented in the corridor of the temple at Ramesvaram. A remarkable bronze group at Conjeevaram has for its central figure a Hindu general, Todar-Mall (c. 1710 A.D.), who commanded the armies of the Nawab of the Carnatic: another excellent group of the members of his family is to be found in the well-known temple of Tirumalai. A group of the Nayaka king Vijayaranga-Chokkanatha (1704-31 A.D.), his queen, his brother and his wife, in the great temple of Srirangam, is made of sandalwood veneered over with flakes of ivory. A Travancore king, Bala-Ramavarman (1761 A.D.), and his nephew are sculptured in a group posted in front of the main shrine of the temple at Suchindram.

The south Indian sculptor was not a flunkey devoting his talents to the immortalizing of the facial lineaments of the rich and the powerful; his chisel was very frequently employed in carving the features of those who, though lowly, were yet endowed richly with the rare virtue of faith. The builder of even a small shrine, a maidservant in a temple, a mere ascetic, a lay worshipper soliciting boons, a devotee who made a gift of some gold for the burning of a perpetual lamp in the temple, the tuneful chanter of a hymn of praise and faith, an undistinguished player on the *vina*, a Captain in the army of the Chola king, the sister of the Captain, the servants of a temple who established the title of their god to certain properties by acts of noble self-sacrifice, a dancing girl who collected funds for building a temple, a foot-soldier who journeyed in faith and hope to the sanctuary which to him was a Jerusalem, a servant who instituted services for the merit of his liege-lord,— these are some of the subjects which have been lovingly chosen and carefully worked at by the sculptors. Divakara, a Kanarese poet of the 9th century A.D., Devasena, the pupil of a preceptor of a Bana king of the same century, Sami-Nirmadi a lady famous for her knowledge of the *sastras*, Isana-Siva-pandita the *guru* of the Chola king Rajaraja I, Kamban, the greatest epic poet of south India (12th century A.D.), Lokabharana-deva a *guru* of a Chalukyan king of that century, Gorakhnath the founder, perhaps, of a well-known *matha* at Kadri,—these are some of the persons whom sculptors honoured by fashioning statues in their image.

If traditions are to be relied on, statues of Ramanuja, the greatest protagonist of south Indian Vaishnavism, were set up in his own lifetime and with his approval at Melkote

                    South Indian Portraits in Stone and Metal

and Sriperumbudur, places associated with his life, and a statue of him (of clay and cloth) was set up on his death over his grave in one of the circuits of the great temple at Srirangam and a shrine was raised over the image. One of his successors, Vedanta-Desika, is said to have fashioned and cast a marvellously accurate likeness of himself so that his title *sarva tantra sva tantra* might stand vindicated. Another successor, Manavala Mahamuni, is said to have given his drinking vessel to his disciples so that they might make an image of him out of it.

These are but a selection from a host of interesting sculptures in stone, metal, wood and other materials, ranging in time from before the opening of the Christian era.

Literary works in the various languages of India do not generally allude to this class of sculptures. A few references in Sanskrit literature are utilised later in discussing the evolution of portrait sculpture. The earliest Tamil literature now available contains indications of the popularity of sculptures portraying human beings; the most outstanding instance is that of consecrating images of the hero and the heroine of the **Silappadikaram,**—a great epic poem not later than the 3rd century A.D. A close examination of the various vernacular literatures of India must bring to light valuable information about the popularity and the progress of portrait-sculpture in the respective areas in which those literatures have grown up.

II

THE ELEMENT OF PORTRAITURE

What justification have we for believing these sculptures to be portraits? Were they mere effigies intended to symbolise certain persons or were they likenesses of those persons and were they executed with the fidelity and the art necessary for genuine portraiture?

Most of these sculptures must have been good portraits: it is unlikely that artists who excelled in every branch of sculpture would have lacked only the genius for portraiture. Mahendravarman I, who prided himself on the exquisiteness of his tastes, and Krishnadevaraya, whose aesthetic accomplishments are too well-known to need recounting, would not have been satisfied with statues which were wanting in the essential quality of faithful likeness. But we must determine whether we have no further or more substantial reasons for believing these sculptures to be portraits.

Only the carved figures are now before us: the originals in flesh and blood have long since passed into dust: the portrait and the subject of portraiture cannot be now placed side by side for comparison. Contemporary pen pictures of none of the persons for whom statues have been set up are now available. If we discovered two or more statues of the same person and compared them with each other in detail, and if we found that though set up at different places, the sculptures are alike in the essential characteristics of figure, feature and expression, we cannot but conclude that they are indubitable portraits. Where we have only one statue, we are driven to base our judgment on such circumstances as the extent to which figures of the members of the same family bear a resemblance to each other or the extent to which the sculptor attempted individualization, or could have succeeded in achieving it.

In seeking to identify the kings who are represented in the two relievos in the Adi-Varaha temple at Mahabalipuram, reliance has been till now placed on a theory that Mahabalipuram, which is also known as Mamallapuram, was founded in the days of the Pallava king, Narasimhavarman I (c. 625-50 A.D.) who was otherwise known as Ma-malla, and that the king named the town after himself.[2] If Mahabalipuram was founded in the days of Narasimhavarman I it is not likely that the relievos were executed before his days or that they represent kings earlier than him. But the theory of the foundation of Mahabalipuram by Narasimhavarman I is entirely gratuitous. There being numerous instances in south India, as elsewhere in the world, of potentates choosing to re-name places after themselves, we have no warrant whatever for assuming that Mahabalipuram owes its existence to Narasimhavarman I: at best, he might have re-named it after himself. Nor is evidence wanting in the Tamil classics to prove that Mamalla-puram

---

2.   Krishna-Sastri, *Two Statues of Pallava Kings* (*ASI. M. 26*); Dr. Jouveau-Dubreuil, *Pallava Antiquities*, i. 64.

was in existence and that it went by that name long before Narasimhavarman I.[3] Once we recognise that the city could have been founded much earlier than that king, we are in a position to discuss without prepossessions the issue as to the identity of the persons pictured in the relievos.[4]

We know that the cave-temples and the *rathas* of Mahabalipuram belong to the days of the Pallava dynasty, that in that part of the country it is only kings of that dynasty who bore the names Simhavishnu and Mahendravarman, and that Mahendravarman I (c. 600-25 A.D.). was the earliest Pallava king to bear that name.[5] The *rathas* and rock-cut temples,— including the temple of Adi-Varaha,—are known to have been constructed by the Pallava kings and a study of the evolution of the architecture of these monuments enables us to declare that they could not be earlier than Simhavishnu (c. 575-600 A.D.) nor later than Paramesvaravarman I (e. 675 A.D.).[6] The Pallava kings between 575 and 675 A.D. are Simhavishnu, Mahendravarman I, Narasimhavarman I, Mahendravarman II and Paramesvaravarman I. From what is known of the motives which underlay the practice of erecting statues, it looks likely that both the kings figured in the Adi-Varaha temple had the temple constructed, or, at least, that one of them had

---

3.   Pandit M. Raghava Aiyangar, *History of the Alvars*, which appeared serially in the *Tamilian's Friend*.

4.   If it be imperative that the foundation,— not the re-naming,— of Mahabalipuram should be assigned to about this time, would it not be almost equally appropriate to ascribe it to Mahendravarman I, he having borne the *biruda, Malla*, as in *Satru-Malla*?

5.   Dr. Jouveau-Dubreuil, *Pallavas*, 35.

6.   Dr. Jouveau-Dubreuil, *Pallava Antiquities*, i. 64.

    South Indian Portraits in Stone and Metal

it constructed and had a figure of his father carved in it in addition to his own. In any event, it is wholly improbable that the actual builder of the temple did not provide a niche for himself and was content with finding niches for his ancestors. The possibilities are, therefore, that the two figures represent one of the three pairs: Simhavishnu and Mahendravarman I, or Mahendravarman I and Narasimhavarman I, or Narasimhavarman I and Mahendravarman II.

Of these kings, Mahendravarman II never ruled; even if he had actually ruled, he could not have taken part in the construction of the temples and *rathas* of Mahabalipuram, for his reign seems to have been very short.[7] It is more than improbable that Narasimhavaram I started constructing the temple and put into it a standing figure of his father and also a figure showing himself not merely seated just opposite his father but also presuming to play the part of *guru* to whom the *chin-mudra* was appropriate. We have, therefore, sufficient justification for believing that Simhavishnu, the seated king, is the father and that Mahendravarman, the standing king, is the son. Further, it being usual to start a series of sculptures from a point to the left of a worshipper entering or facing the temple, the position of Simhavishnu's statue at such a point in this temple suggests that Simhavishnu was a predecessor and not a successor of the Mahendravaman in the opposite panel. The two sculptures must represent respectively Simhavishnu and his son Mahendravarman I.

Against this conclusion have been adduced arguments which are not very convincing. Among the names of the Pallava kings we find two—Simhavishnu and Narasimhavarman,—which

---

7. *Ib.* 1. 40; *Pallavas*, 42.

could be treated as synonymous and, indeed, we do find them so used in the case of a later king of this line,—Narasimhavarman II, who bore a second name, Narasimhavishnu.[8] But, Narasimhavarman I was never called Simhavishnu and we cannot build a positive hypothesis on the mere possibility of an *alias* when we have no concrete instance to support it. Other arguments are based on palaeographic and architectural considerations, but, the reign of Mahendravarman I being admittedly the starting point of a period of transition both in palaeography and architecture, very little weight deserves to be attached to indications not unequivocally pointing to definite conclusions.[9] The admission has been made that 'the

8. *SII* i. 10, 110-24; Fleet, *Dynasties of the Kanarese Districts*, (2nd ed.), 330, Fleet maintains, on the basis of an inscription at Badami, that Narasimhavarman I was called Narasimha-vishnu (IA. ix. 100; but he makes admissions (in note 20 on that page) which make the theory rather weak. The main grounds on which he makes the identification are that this inscription speaks of a Pallava conquest of Vatapi and that we know of only one Pallava king, Narasimhavarman I, to whom the achievement is to be credited. The possibility of Vatapi having been taken by Paramesvaravarman I also (see A. Rangasvami-Sarasvati's paper on the Kodumbalur Chiefs in the *Vijayanagaram Maharajah's College Magazine* for July 1923, pp. 206-9, *cf.* MER. 1908: 88: 88) shows that there could be no inherent improbability in a similar claim being established in the case of Simhavishnu as well.

9. Krishna-sastri, in his memoir. *Two Statues of Pallava Kings* (ASI. M. 26), bases indeed his argument in identification of the Simhavishnu relief as a portrait of Narasimhavarman, on the fact that this is a period of transition. But we have no reason to hold that the transition did not start in the days of Mahendravarman I himself. Indeed, Dr. Jouveau-Dubreuil is compelled to distinguish two distinct palaeographic styles in Mahendravarman I's days (*Pallava Antiquities*, i. 39). If the squatting lions at the base of the Adi-Varaha temple argue for a date

                        South Indian Portraits in Stone and Metal

monuments of Mahabalipuram very much resemble those of Mahendra', though it has been qualified by the statement that the general aspect of the sculptures is, yet, 'altered.'[10] This change does not seem to be so marked indeed as not to admit of the explanation that it is due to the natural evolution of sculptural methods in the course of the reign of a king who was a great builder. The figure of Mahendravarman I in the

---

posterior to him (*Ib.* i. 59), the *dvara-palakas* so carved as to present a fall-front view speak for a period contemporary with him. (*Ib.* i 60) Even if we assume that Narasimhavarman I is represented in the relief, the absence of likenesses of any of his successors in that temple shows that the temple must have been completed within his reign. What probability could there be in a theory which requires Mahendravarman I to have started carving the sculptures in the temple, including that of himself and the *dvara palakas*, but to have left it to Narasimhavarman I to carve the pillars with the squatting lions at the base and the labels giving the names of the kings? We can attach no special importance to this temple being associated with the name of Paramesvaravarman (*vide* Krishna-Sastri's *Two Statues of Pallava Kings*, 8); we have already seen that the sculptures of kings could not have been carved by him, and the association with Paramesvaravarman might have sprung up, if there be substance in the suggestion that the temple was originally carved for Siva, at the time when an image of Vishnu was installed in the *sanctum*. Even Krishna-Sastri does not venture to claim that the characteristics of the inscriptions and the sculptures of this temple indicate that they are to be attributed clearly and indisputably to the days of Narasimhavarman I in preference to those of Mahendravarman I. Perhaps it may also be pointed out that the features of the Simhavishnu of the Adi-Varaha temple are very different from those of the figure in the Dharmaraja *ratha* which has been tentatively identified here as a likeness of Narasimhavarman I.

10. I am sure that Dr. Jouveau-Dubreuil would have admitted that the sculptures at Mahabalipuram dated from at least Mahendravarman I had he been inside the Adi-Varaha temple and seen the statues in it.

relief seems to show him turned forty. If we take it that the Trichinopoly cave and other similar temples were constructed by him in the earlier part of his reign, and that the Adi-Varaha temple was completed late in the reign, there should be no difficulty in imputing the change in the aspect of the Mahabalipuram sculptures to the evolution natural in the case of a rapidly growing art.[11]

Perhaps Mahendravarman I constructed the temple and cut niches in it for himself and his father,— a course for which we find a parallel in the Nanaghat group,— or, perhaps, his father Simhavishnu started the work and he himself completed it, and so niches were assigned to both of them as builders of the temple. In any event, the statue of Mahendravarman I must have been carved in his own lifetime and that of Simhavishnu within a few years of his death. Mahendravarman I who took credit for being a *Vichitra-chitta*[12] was not likely to have allowed figures to have passed muster for likenesses of himself and his father had he not been satisfied that they were faithful as portraits. The similarities in the features of the two figures are not greater, and are certainly not less, than those usually found in the case of a father and a son.

In the rock-cut cave at Sittannavasal, which has become deservedly famous for its ancient frescos, a painting of a head on one of the pillars bears so close a resemblance to the

---

11.   Dr. Jouveau-Dubreuil, *Pallava Antiquities*, i. 75. If the other statue represents Narasimhavarman I, not much time could have elapsed since the death of Mahendravarman I and it is, therefore, likely that Mahendravarman's statue also is a faithful portrait.

12.   Dr. G. Jouveau-Dubreuil, Conjeevaram Inscription of Mahendravarman I, 3.

                        South Indian Portraits in Stone and Metal

sculptured head of Mahendravarman at Mahabalipuram that the resemblance cannot be set down to accident. The cave being associated in many ways with Mahendravarman I, the painting has been taken to be a portrait of that king. To use the resemblance to support the contention that portraiture was a well-established art in Mahendravarman's days is, strictly speaking, to argue in a circle, but still we can neither overlook the resemblance nor evade the natural inference.

If the resemblance in figure and features between the statues of persons related closely to each other may be taken as proof of successful portraiture, we may point to the group of the Chola captain and his sister, to the group of the three Yalahanka brothers, and to the group of the Travancore king and his nephew as being excellent portraits; in the first of these groups there is an unmistakable identity in even the expression, and in the last of them there is palpable resemblance between the features of the uncle and the nephew.

In the gallery of Nayaka kings at Madura, we may closely study the features of five generations of a family. Every one of the statues is carved in the standing posture with the hands joined in salutation: there are practically no variations in the style of dress or the type of jewellery which each person is shown to have worn. In spite of these common features, every one of the statues looks different from the others. An excellent estimate of them, based on a careful study of the individual variations and the general effect, runs thus: 'The aim of that unknown Dravidian Phidias who carved them was to reproduce the previous kings of Madura as they were, not idealised as sculptures did. And he attains his aim indeed. . .

They are true portraits.' And again: 'The statues are different from each other, but among the individual differences of each statue a general likeness is to be seen. They constitue a collection of portraits of the ten first Nayaks of Madura which any museum would be proud of.' How successful the sculptor was in making true portraits of these sculptures is brought home to us when we study the statue of Tirumala Nayaka,— the one that stands last in the gallery: 'Naturally Tirumala Nayak's statue is still more elaborated than all those of his predecessors. We may affirm that it is the most faithful in representing the individual features of the royal constructor of that precious *mantapam* and they are very striking indeed. Tirumala is shown there as the heir of all the bodily characteristics of the Nayak family, but all these characteristics are developed in him in an extraordinary manner, as showing practically that all the good qualities of his ancestors were combined in him and carried to a supreme degree of perfection. His broad jaw, his powerful shoulders, his tremendous hips, his strong gigantic legs and even his protuberant abdomen, bulging out over the belt, are some of those features which we may see in almost all the preceding statues and are here carried to an extreme of development. These bodily characteristics in the statue of Tirumala are but a manifestation of the spiritual qualities inherited also from his forefathers'.[13]

The line of statues begins with Visvanatha (c. 1529-64 A.D.), the real founder of this dynasty, and ends with Tirumala himself (1623-52 A.D.). Between the death of the founder of the dynasty and the accession of the king who had the statues set up, barely sixty years elapsed and only four

------

13.   Father H. Heras, in *QJMS*. xv. 209-18.

generations intervened. We may take it, therefore, that very little difficulty could have been felt either in ascertaining the order in which the kings followed each other or in gathering from reliable sources an adequate idea of at least the more characteristic of the physical features of each of the kings. So highly individualised are these figures that we cannot but assume that whoever fashioned them must have had before him faithful portraits of every member of this family.

A study of the family groups of Ramesvaram, Pattisvaram and Srirangam makes it obvious that the sculptors were masters of the art of portraiture and that their craftsmanship was inferior only to that of the sculptors who worked for Tirumala Nayaka.

It is in the 7th century A.D. that we first have mention of more than one representation of the same person—a statue for Mahendravarman I at Trichinopoly and a relievo at Mahabalipuram. But we do not now have two portraits of the same person earlier than Vishnuvardhana, unless the fresco in the Sittannavasal cave represents Mahendravarman I, in which case we have two portraits of Mahendravarman I as well,—the one a sculpture and the other a painting.

The stone figure of Vishnuvardhana, decayed as it is, does not differ much from the statue of bronze: short in height, rough in build and grave of countenance, the two figures agree closely in spite of the difference in the material, the variation in the pose and the departures in drapery and ornamentation.

Statues or relievos of Krishnadevaraya, the great Vijayanagara emperor, are known to have been placed at Tirumalai, Chidambaram, Srisailam and Vijayanagar. We cannot identify his figure at Srisailam with certainty and the face of the carving at Vijayanagar has been greatly damaged. We are thus driven to rely on? A comparison of the Tirumalai and the Chidambaram sculptures.

The Tirumalai group of Krishnadevaraya and his two queens is highly instructive. To judge from the characters in which the names are engraved, (on the right shoulder in each case), the images must have been set up during the lifetime of the king. Further, the statue of the king looks that of a well-trained athlete, and we know from the account of a Portuguese chronicler, Dominogo Paes, that Krishnadevaraya was 'a strong man fond of outdoor sports' and regular in taking physical exercise; he would 'drink a three-quarter pint of gingelly oil before daylight and then take exercise until he sweated out all the oil.'[14] The statue cannot, therefore, be merely a conventional representation: it must have been a good portrait. The statues of the emperor and his queens, however, seem to agree so closely in the features and even the expression that one questions oneself whether the statues do not represent a brother and his sisters. Knowing as we do definitely that Krishnadevaraya and his two queens came from three different families in no wise related to one another, it is not easy to account for the resemblance. Perhaps the taste of Krishnadevaraya, which we know to have been fastidious, led him to choose for wives two ladies whose features and expression answered to his standards of beauty, and it is not altogether remarkable that the features and the expression agreed with his own. Or, perhaps, the queens could not, owing to the custom of seclusion, give sittings to the sculptors, who must, in consequence, have been forced to rely on unfaithful

---

14.   *MER.* 1904: 4: 9.

                    South Indian Portraits in Stone and Metal

and uncritical accounts of the appearance of the queens or to give free rein to their fancy. Or, it may be that the sculptors followed the age-old Indian artistic tradition of concentrating their attention on the principal figure in a group to the utter neglect of the subsidiary figures. If, however, after Mahendravarman I another *Vichitrachitta* sat on the throne of any south Indian kingdom, it was Krishnadevaraya, and we cannot believe that he would have allowed figures to be set up as likenesses which lacked the essential qualification of being good portraits. We have to conclude that the statue of Krishnadevaraya was certainly a portrait and that perhaps the statues of the queens were also good portraits.

The Chidambaram statue may not be compared with that at Tirumalai. Though the violence of some vandal has damaged the nose of the statue at Chidambaram, it is yet possible to see that the features are those of a person determined in will and cultivated in tastes: the sculpture clearly shows a person strong in limb and graceful in carriage. These qualities of the Chidambaram statue answer to all the details we have of Krishnadevaraya and we may take the statue to be a fairly accurate, though perhaps not an artistically adequate, portrait of that emperor. The Chidambaram statue would seem to show Krishnadevaraya grown a little older than in the group at Tirumalai,—a little flabbier in muscle, a little fuller about the waist, a little mellower in expression. Both the statues show him engaged in worship, but while in the Tirumalai statue we have an exemplification of the frigidity of devotion, the Chidambaram statue stands in illustration of its freedom. If we isolated the copper-statue of Krishnadevaraya from the Tirumalai group and placed it alongside of the stone statue at Chidambaram and compared the two statues, making allowance for the differences in the material, the pose and the expression, and also for the mutilation of the Chidambaram figure, there can be little doubt that they will be found good likenesses of the same person.

Two statues of Kanthirava-Narasa-Odayar, king of Mysore, are known,— one at Seringapatam and another at Mysore,— but the latter is fashioned too crudely to be compared with the former which is very elaborately executed in bronze.

At least four statues of Tirumala Nayaka of Madura are known—at Madura, Srivilliputtur, Tirupparankunram and Alagarkoyil. The resemblance between them is striking: it would almost seem as if replicas of the statue at Madura had been made and set up at the other places. The sculptors who fashioned these statues were masters indeed of their art. The queens who are sculptured beside the kings of the Madura gallery might have been sketched from the life, but perhaps they too were treated as uninteresting subsidiary figures and no efforts might have been made to ensure that they were portrayed with fidelity.

The two statues we have of the wife of Govinda-Dikshita show that the sculptors who fashioned them must have studied their subject with care.

The resemblance between the sculptured piece known as Mangammal's minister and the portrait of (Dalavay) Ramappayya painted in the ceiling nearby is striking, but we cannot be certain that the subject portrayed was the same in both cases.

          South Indian Portraits in Stone and Metal

The Todar-Mall groups at Conjeevaram and Tirumalai should have served admirably the purposes of a comparative study, but, as ill-luck would have it, two of the members of the Tirumalai group are damaged, and another, perhaps the statue of Todar-Mall himself, has disappeared, and even tradition is not clear about the identity of the surviving figures.

But the majority of the statues are those set up singly and at only one place to one subject and in most of such cases we can only hazard a guess that the sculptures are portraits. The hazard, however, is not great where we have to decide whether faithful likeness would have been a characteristic of the statues set up to such eminent persons as Parantaka II and his queen by their daughter, or to king Rajaraja I by the manager of the temple built by that king, or to queen Sembiyan Mahadevi by herself or by her relations, or to queen Solamadevi by her step-son, the great Rajendra I, or to Kulottunga III by a feudatory. Not only do these sculptures belong to one of the most noteworthy of the periods of south Indian art but they represent kings and queens of one of the most powerful dynasties of south India, who would certainly not have been content with statues which were mere effigies.

For the other statues, however, we have to rely on the individualization of the figures and features and on the fact that not one of those sculptures bears even a faint resemblance to any of the others. Even the man of ordinary means was not likely to have put himself to the expense of a statue were he not confident that the sculptor would portray him truly. We may presume that sculptures of this class too were not wanting in the essential quality of portraiture, for the south Indian sculptor has from the first produced sculptures of no mean merit as portraits. Portraiture was no *pons asinorum* to the south Indian artist.

III

✦

THE CRAVING FOR PORTRAITURE

How are we to account for the *penchant* which the south Indian has undoubtedly had for centuries for carving and installing sculptures which he intended to be statues? No answer will be correct or comprehensive till every type of portrait sculpture has been studied and every motive inducing men to set up statues has been explored.

We may attain to a truer appreciation of the course of evolution of portrait sculpture if we realised that what might at first sight appear to be compelling motives do not sometimes come into play at all. Two illustrations should be enough.

Drona declined, according to the *Mahabharata*, to receive Ekalavya as a pupil. Nothing discouraged, Ekalavya 'made Drona out of clay,' and, worshipping the clay reverently as if it were a preceptor in flesh and blood, practised warlike weapons before it and attained to a remarkable proficiency in their use.[15] The passage leaves it ambiguous whether Ekalavya turned artist and set himself the preliminary task of blessing

---

15.   Mahabharata, Adi-parva, (Sambhava-), sect, 134.

                      South Indian Portraits in Stone and Metal

the clay with the features of Drona; had he done so, he might have turned out a good artist but learned little of the science of war. Ekalavya, however, kept Drona so steadily before his mind's eye that he had no need for more than an amorphous lump of clay to stand for Drona before his physical eye.

In parts of south India, as in some other parts of the world, a fond believer in magic, anxious to rid himself of his neighbour, fancies it would all be to the good if the neighbour should die, say, of colic, and he straight-away engages the most reputed practitioner of the black art. The magician carves an effigy of human shape out of a piece of wood a few inches long, mutters some spells over it, drives a nail into the stomach of the effigy, and chants more spells over effigy and nail. Where luck aids the imposture and the neighbour dies, the art of magic scores, much to the profit of the practitioner of the art. No such effigy, however, is found carved into a real likeness of the person against whom the magic has been directed, obviously because no magician has persuaded himself that he could improve the potency of his spells by improving a mere effigy into a passable portrait.

If some motives fail to be productive of portraits, there are others which are prolific, though they may not all be equally fertile.

The motive behind a statue may often be discovered by determining when, where and by whom it was installed.

Some statues were set up by the subjects themselves, but anyone could, it seems, have statues set up for himself or for anyone else. A Chola queen had an image of her husband carved and a Chola princess had images of her parents set up. A Satakarni queen had a group fashioned to represent herself, her husband, father-in- law, father and sons. Rajendra installed a bronze of his step-mother. Tirumala Nayaka set up a gallery of likenesses of his ancestors and a prime-minister of his dynasty. A sister presented a bronze of her brother and, evidently, followed it up with one of herself. A feudatory set up statues both of his father-in-law and of his overlord, the Vijayanagara king, in addition to his own. An officer set up bronzes of himself and a colleague. Disciples consecrated statues to their preceptors.

Restrictions were not placed on setting up images of the same person in a number of places. Portraits of Mahendravarman I were carved in the rock-cut caves of Trichinopoly and Mahabalipuram, and a portrait was painted at Sittannavasal: sculptures representing Krishnadevaraya were placed at Tirumalai, Chidambaram and Srisailam: statues of the members of the Todar-Mall family are found at Tirumalai and Conjeevaram: Ramanuja s effigy was set up at both Melkote and at Sriperumbudur.

Statues accumulate under one roof through a variety of causes. Numerous devotees contribute towards the construction of temples like those of Tiruvaduturai or Konerirajapuram or of edifices such as the architectural appendages of the Amaravati *stupa* and devotees who can afford it put in figures of themselves. Kings of the Pallava dynasty in the 7th century A.D. think it their duty to embellish Mahabalipuram and they leave behind them marks of their activity by including their own likenesses among the sculptures which they get carved out of the rocks scattered pell-mell on the surf-beaten shore. The builder of a temple, or it may be the builder of an extension, has a relievo or other sculpture carved in it to

South Indian Portraits in Stone and Metal

represent himself; another devotee builds a minor shrine or repairs the old temple and instals a figure of himself; a third devotee seeks to distinguish himself over others by setting up a full-fledged statue in his own image, perhaps getting permission for it by valuable gifts to the temple, and he is in turn emulated by others: thus accumulates in that temple a series of sculptures representing unrelated individuals. A temple becomes popular at one time or another in its history and worshippers who are anxious to leave permanent memorials of their devotion set up statues of themselves in the attitude of worship. One member of a family—it is a dynasty of potentates in the Tirumalai temple,—starts paying his devotions to the deity of a temple, and his descendants and other members of his family follow in his wake, treating the god of the temple as their *kula-devata*, with the result that every important member of the family finds for himself a niche, however small, in that temple. Or, a king, such as a Nayaka of Madura, becomes a passionate devotee of the deity of a temple,—often the principal one in his capital, as in the case of Madura,—and makes lavish gifts of jewellery to the image and extensive grants of land to the temple and starts making architectural additions on a grand scale. When the work is complete, he sets up at least a statue of himself and, if more ambitious, he instals statues of his predecessors as well. All of them are mindful of the transitoriness of physical life and the shortness of the period in which they could in their proper person keep worshipping the deity enshrined in the temple. Being anxious to prolong their devotion beyond even this life, at least so long as temple and carved-stone or cast-metal would endure, they instal statues of themselves in the

South Indian Portraits in Stone and Metal   33

temple, their hands joined in salutation: they have gone their way and the world has not known them for over a thousand years, and yet their statues now stand in the temples rendering salutation which in the thousand years has lost no whit in sincerity. Some devotees have a fascination for burning 'perpetual lamps' in temples for their merit and they have a partiality for setting themselves up in such form that, though turned into stone or metal, they could yet be seen engaged in service to the deity ever afterwards. So, instead of having the hands of the sculpture joined in salutation, they put a lamp into its hands, so that the figure, generally of metal, might stand for all time holding a burning lamp before the deity for the illumination of the shrine. A similar motive is exemplified in the statuettes of the Vijayaranga-Chokkanatha group which stand as if they wielded fly- whisks.

The builder of a *stupa* or a temple is anxious to commemorate his having accomplished the pious task he had set himself and carves a figure of himself in it. A king desires to enhance the attractions of the chief shrine of his capital by architectural additions to it and takes the opportunity of carving out immortality for himself in stone in his own image. King Bala-Ramavarman protects with, uplifted sword the sacred precincts of the Suchindram temple, Kulottunga III protects the holy fane of Kalahasti with a dagger held unsheathed, and 'Raja-rajendra-chola of the Big Temple' of Tanjore acts as escort to the image of the deity of the temple he had built, whenever the image is taken out in procession. A general, Todar-Mall, brings the deity of Conjeevaram back from exile and either commemorates the event, or it is commemorated, by the installation of statues of him and his family in the temple. Queen Sembiyan Mahadevi

                    South Indian Portraits in Stone and Metal

builds a temple in the name of her husband, king Gandaraditya, and she carves in it a relief of him. Princess Kundavai has such respect for her parents that she instals images of them in a temple which her brother built. Rajaraja seems to have sanctioned the inclusion of a likeness of his priest among the images set up in that temple. Even kings and queens desire to stand for ever before the deity, performing services such as those of waving fly-whisks, and they take pride in representing themselves as engaged in such services. One devotee portrays himself asking for boons. Other devotees found endowments for twilight lamps and place statues of themselves in the temple.

Anxious to secure the salvation of her brother, a lady places a bronze likeness of him in a temple and, later, she places a likeness of herself in the temple in the evident hope that the Lord will be merciful to those who stand suing for ever for His grace. A tower is erected on the spot where a certain person planted a spear and some persons are figured in it holding spears; Figures of religious men, *jīyars* and *ekangis*, who immolated themselves by falling from a temple *gopura* in protest against the tyranny of a chief are, some twenty years later, carved in stone and set up in the temple by grateful citizens.

Religious fervour blends with every one of these motives, and, every figure, not excluding those which do not join the hands in salutation, is eloquently expressive of deep and strong devotion.

The predominance of this element of devotion explains why many of the portraits in stone are executed very crudely. The excellence of even the early sculptures such as those at Amaravati or Mahabalipuram precludes the suspicion that the crudeness might have been due to want of sculptural skill.

The prominence sought to be given to the Satakarni statue in its setting in the *stupa* of Amaravati and the grandeur of groups such as the one at Madura make it improbable that temple-builders felt no craving: to put their devotion into arresting shape. The evidence we have of the power and the wealth of the Satakarnis, the Pallavas and the Nayakas, for instance, must warn us against assuming that the lack of finish was due to the necessity for observing parsimony. Knowing as we do how lavish Krishnadevaraya was, we cannot pretend that the comparative crudity of his statue at Chidambaram must have been due to reasons of economy. Indeed, the crude portraits are often found in temples of liberal dimensions and of excellent workmanship. The explanation seems to lie in the circumstance that many, if not most of the temple builders, while desirous of putting in effigies of themselves as devotees, were not so wanting in the humility of true devotion as to raise costly and grandiose monuments to themselves. It was not the pride of having built the temple but the zeal for keeping for ever in the presence of the deity in an unceasing salutation or engaged in interminable service, like the holding of a light or the wielding of a fly-whisk, that prompted the builder to instal his own effigy in the temple. For this purpose it was immaterial whether the devotee's figure was an artistically perfect portrait or was merely carved into a rough resemblance to the human shape.

The instinct for decorative effect must certainly have played an important part in disposing men and women to set up portrait sculptures: the influence of this instinct is clear in the finely-modelled statue of the Satakarni of the Amaravati *stupa*, in the beautiful relievos of the Mahabalipuram rock-

                    South Indian Portraits in Stone and Metal

cut temple, in the lovely bronzes of Sembiyan Mahadevi and Solamadevi and in the elaborately-chased bronze statuette of Kanthirava-Narasa-0dayar and in the of grouping of statues in portrait galleries. Evidence of the vogue of decorative statues is to be found in early Tamil literature. But no portrait would have been installed for mere decorative effect, for, if decoration was the only motive, the element of portraiture would obviously have been superfluous. The instinct for decoration must, therefore, have been subordinate to the desire for portraiture.

The evidence we have so far had of the prevalence of portraiture in every medium indicates the total absence of prohibitions against the fashioning of portraits or the setting up of portrait sculptures. Though Jatavarman Sundara-Pandya I was a lavish donor to the great temple of Srirangam he seems to have been denied the privilege of setting up a statue to himself in that temple. The chronicle recording the incident states no reasons for the refusal; much less does it ground it on any authoritative dicta prohibiting portrait sculpture. The refusal must, therefore, have been due to some special circumstances of the case of which we have no knowledge. But, occasionally we find portraiture looked at askance. Though most of the Vaishnava hagiologists who speak of images in the likeness of the great preceptors say that they were installed while these preceptors were yet alive, one of the hagiologists states that Ramanuja felt himself growing weak when an image of him was being consecrated at his birth-place: the suggestion seems to be that the weakness was due to Ramanuja's 'powers' being transplanted from his body to the image. Another hagiologist records that though Vedanta-Desika made his own statue, he had it stowed away because of its supreme perfection as a likeness. Sukra, a writer of authority, enunciates the dicta that 'the images of gods yield happiness to men and lead to heaven, but those of men lead away from heaven and yield grief'[16] and that 'the images of men, even if well- formed, are never for human good.'[17] Sukra's injunction against the making of images of men is quite positive, while the statements about Ramanuja and Vedanta-Desika reflect a belief that it is hazardous to allow a statue to be exhibited or consecrated in the lifetime of the subject. Sukra's condemnation of even 'well-formed' statues points to the inference that 'ill-formed' ones were assumed to work evil: the story about Vedanta-Desika shows that it was believed that evil would result from the very perfection of the portraiture. The suggestion against 'ill-formed' statues must be due to the belief, popular all over the world, that a thing of evil aspect is a potent source of evil. So too, the apprehension of evil from even the beauty of an object has its source in the equally vulgar belief in such an object attracting the malevolence of the evil eye.

It deserves to be noted, however, that there is no direct authority in any of the scriptures against the installing of portrait statues, and it is not without significance that the earliest of the indubitable examples of portrait sculpture is the series of relievos at Nanaghat executed in the 2nd century B.C. in commemoration of so orthodox a ceremonial as a vedic sacrifice, and that so early as the 7th century A.D. a statue of Mahendravarman I was placed next to the idol of the deity in a temple, the very citadel of orthodoxy.

16.	*Sukra-Niti*, ('Sacred Books of the Hindus'), IV. iv. 154-5.

17.	*Ib.*, IV. iv. 158.

	South Indian Portraits in Stone and Metal

IV

❧

STATUES FOR WORSHIP

Many of the portrait sculptures were set up in the lifetime of the subjects themselves, as is evident from the inscriptions beside the Nanaghat relievo and as is expressly stated in respect of the image of Mahendravarman I at Trichinopoly and of the bronzes which the devotees of Annur, Tirukkannapuram and Kalahasti gave away along with their gifts for perpetual lamps. A fine story in the *Mahabharata* relates that Dhritarashtra, furious with Bhima, sought to hug and crush him to death, when Krishna taking advantage of Dhritarashtra's blindness, dragged Bhima away and thrust an iron statue of Bhima into the villainous arms of Dhritarashtra, and that so powerful was the hug which the statue received that it broke to pieces in the furious embrace.[18] This statue must obviously have been set up in Bhima's lifetime. An ancient Buddhist legend says, that king Bimbisara had an image of the Buddha made in sandalwood in the lifetime of the Buddha. Only the love of the miraculous

---

18.   *Mahabharata, Stri-parva, sect.* 12,

makes the *Divyavadana* say that so ineffable were the features of the Buddha that no artist succeeded in portraying them.[19]

Numerous sculptures, however, were set up after the death of the subjects of portraiture. In the Satakarni group at Nanaghat were included two kings who were dead when the group was carved. Gandaraditya was dead when his wife had an image of him carved in a temple which she built. The statue in memory of Parantaka II was installed by his daughter many years after his death. The image of the Chola captain was lovingly offered to a temple by his fond sister after his death. Metallic images of the servants of the temple of Kidaramkondan were set up after they had lost their lives in defence of the property belonging to the temple. Statues of the nine predecessors of Tirumala Nayaka were set up only when he built the famous 'Pudu-Mandapam' at Madura. The citizens of Srirangam set up likenesses of persons who were dead some twenty years.

Were any of the statues worshipped or were any of them intended for worship? Portrait sculptures being mostly found in temples and the subjects of portraiture being usually represented as devotees, one would suppose that they cannot become objects of worship; their position in temples as representations of devotees should itself stand in the way of their becoming, in their turn, objects of worship. Did mere devotees who signalized themselves by their gifts or their architectural activities acquire such sanctity as entitled them to be worshipped? However sincerely the poets of the *bhakti-marga*, 'the path of devotion,' described themselves as devotees

---

19.   See Prof. A. Foucher, Beginnings of Buddhist Art, 18.

                                    South Indian Portraits in Stone and Metal

unto devotees, it is unthinkable that in a temple and in the presence of the deity they would have chosen to offer worship to the statue of, say, the Chola captain, whose place in the temple was due to no personal merits but to the anxiety of his sister for the well-being of his soul.

If a powerful chief had his own image installed in the huge temple which he raised or repaired, the humble devotee whose limited means compelled him to be less demonstrative set up a pillar in modest commemoration of making a gift to the temple or of founding some pious services, and on a face of the pillar he had his god carved above and himself below.[20] Votive monuments of this type are by no means rare. Was it to ensure the merit of the gift reaching the true donor that Hemadri (c.1270 A.D.) said that the merit of making a gift is enhanced by adding to the gift an image of the donor himself?

The statues of Mahendravarman I in the rock-cut temple at Trichinopoly and of Rajaraja I in the great temple of Tanjore, which seem to have been set up in those temples in the lifetime of the respective kings,— perhaps in the holy of holies and next to the *linga*,[21] — could not have been placed there for worship: those kings were no more than the builders of the temples and there was no reason whatever why their images should be worshipped or offerings be made to them. The devotee of Annur who dedicated some of his servants to the service of the temple, gave gold for a lamp and set up a statue of himself and his wife is not known to have made any provision for offerings to the statues. When

---

20.   For instance, see illustration on p. 47.

21.   For a parallel, see illustration on p. 44.

a person set up an image of himself he did so in proof of his abiding devotion and not with a view to worship being offered to himself. If his image was placed next to the idol of the deity of the temple, and even in the sanctuary, it was not because the devotee claimed for himself a rank next below the deity but because he was eager to post himself beside his god so that he may acquire merit by engaging in unending adoration of the deity or in perpetual service to the idol. There would have been, however, no appropriateness in a devotee setting up a statue to represent himself if he did not make it a portrait. Unless his statue had the qualities of a portrait it would not have shown that it was he who was so devoted to his god as to desire to stand in perpetual adoration and service before him.

But, a number of images of human beings are worshipped in every temple in south India, with as much *eclat* as the idol of the deity to whom the temple is dedicated and shrines have been built in the bigger temples for the accommodation of these idols. The *Alvars* of the Vaishnavas and the *Nayanmar* of the Saivites and the *Acharyas* of not only these two sects but of other sects as well have images set up to them either in temples dedicated to the deity of the sect on in separate shrines. The places where these saints or preceptors were born or where they were laid to rest or where they had carried on their ministry became places of pilgrimage. Niches were assigned to them in every temple of their persuasion, and, if the worshippers were sufficiently rich and zealous, shrines were built and worship was offered to them with as much ceremonial as to the deity himself.

                            South Indian Portraits in Stone and Metal

The deep and steadfast religiousness of the Indian has led him to place not only the saint but also the preceptor on a par almost with his god. But the worship of their images is due, not to their being portraits but to their being images of religious personalities. If, for example, the offering of worship to the images of the sixty-three saints of the Siva temples in the Tamil country depended on their being portraits, very few of them, indeed, would be eligible for worship.

The worshipping of the images of the saints and the preceptors is easy of explanation. The worship is only an exaggerated form of the respect which a son shows to his father or a disciple to his preceptor. Respect has deepened and grown into worship.

But we have evidence of worship having been offered to images of persons whom one would have considered by no means eligible for such distinction. We have irrefragable evidence of provision having been made for offerings to statues of mere lay men, irrespective of whether they were of high or low station in life, though it is not till a late date that for the first time we come across a record of the practice. An inscription of the early years of the 11th century A.D. seems to say that the assembly of a village founded by the Chola queen, Sembiyan Mahadevi, and named by her after herself, made grants of land for offerings to an image of that queen set up in a temple which she had built in that village: the grants were made about 1019 A.D.,[22] while the queen had died about 1001 A.D.[23] An inscription recounting the provision

---

22.   *MER.*, 1926: 481 of 1925; *Ib* 1926: 85.

23.   Ib., 1926: 105: 22.

which the sister of Rajaraja I made for offerings to the images of her deceased parents is very clear: it sets out in detail the various kinds of food-offerings that had to be made and even in what quantities and how often a day. A form which worship often took was the burning of lamps in the presence of the images, and we have epigraphical confirmation of the practice in at least two inscriptions which record the grant of land for burning a lamp before the statue of Rajaraja I and another before the statue of his *guru*,—statues of both of them having been set up in the great temple of Tanjore. Offerings were made to the statues set up to the valiant and self-sacrificing devotees of Kidaramkondan.

How are we to explain the making of offerings to statutes of these human personages? Sembiyan Mahadevi and Rajaraja's parents were mere kings and queens,— though distinguished by their surpassing piety and devotion. Were offerings made to them because of their royalty? That cannot be, for offerings were made to sculptures of men drawn from the ranks of the commonalty as is obvious from the worship offered to the servants of the temple of Kidaramkondan. If statues of king and commoner could equally be worshipped, the *raison d'etre* of the worship must be sought for elsewhere than in the social position of the object of worship. The question propounded here cannot be answered except in the light of some facts to which it is necessary to advert.

Except in the case of a religious preceptor like Ramanuja whose image might have been worshipped in his own lifetime at Melkote and Sriperumbudur, we know of no instance of the image of a living person having been made an object of worship. The image of Rajaraja I, for instance, was obviously

　　　South Indian Portraits in Stone and Metal

set up in his lifetime, but no sign of worship is visible till his death. So too, the provision for the worship of the image of Sembiyan Mahadevi seems to have been made only after her death. The just inference would seem to be that though an image may be set up to a person still alive, no worship would be offered to the image so long as the person was in the land of the living, but that on his death it would become a fit object of worship. We may take it that offerings to a statue were made only when it was set up to the dead; at any rate, offerings were not made till the death of the person portrayed in the statue. Worship must have been offered only to the statues of the dead,— except possibly in the case of saints and preceptors. As has been already explained, the worship of saints and preceptors when they are still alive is only a development of the salutation made to a venerable senior,— the formalities and courtesies of salutation being emphasised and dignified into a ritual of worship. We may, therefore, take it that true worship is offered only to the images of the dead.

What, then, is the connection between the worship of a statue and the death of its subject?

V

MEMORIAL STONES

To understand why a statue should be worshipped only on the death of its subject, we may begin by studying a type of monument of which frequent mention is made in early Tamil literature. When a warrior of prowess died, a stone was set up on end, a spear and a shield were planted near it, and a palisade was raised around so as to enclose an area not much larger than an elephant's footprint. Occasionally, the name of the hero was engraved on the stone along with an account of his achievements. The stone was then decked with garlands and peacock feathers; it was anointed with honey: lamps were kept burning in its presence and incense and sacrifices were offered to it. Even passers-by would raise their hands to it in worship.

The earliest Tamil works treat at length of the ceremonies which accompanied the setting up of hero-stones. Prominent mention is made of building a temple for the hero-stone and of installing the stone in it, of the stone being honoured with sacrifices, of eulogies being sung in its honour and of even boons being prayed for at its hands.

 South Indian Portraits in Stone and Metal

The most famous and the earliest of Tamil epics, the *Silappadikaram*, narrates how a king went on an expedition to the Himalayas for a stone which he could carve into an image of a lady who, being a pattern of chastity, had given up her life when her husband was killed, how he built a temple at his capital and installed the stone in it,— perhaps after working it into an image,— and how he obtained boons from the petrified lady. An image of the husband too seems to have been installed in the temple.

Though, at the present day, hero-stones are exceedingly rare in the land in which Tamil is spoken, they are found in countless numbers in the Telugu and the Kanarese countries. Usually the hero-stone bears three bands of sculptures; the lowest band depicts a battle in which the hero fights valiantly; the middle one shows him on the way to paradise, and the topmost one pictures him enjoying the sweets of Elysium. Occasionally, the hero is portrayed alone, in war-like gait, brandishing his weapons, or he rides a horse at full gallop. Inscriptions recording the name of the hero and his valorous exploits are often incised on the stone. From the inscriptions, we gather that grants of land were sometimes made for maintaining daily services in honour of these heroes and that often the lands were freed from liability for the customary imposts.

Stones of this type are found set up not only to those who fell in battle but also to ascetics who burnt themselves to death, to faithful subjects who killed themselves on the death of their king and to persons who starved themselves and forsook life,— indeed to those who treated life as dust and gave it up with resolution. Even beasts which lost their lives in acts of bravery were commemorated with memorial stones. We know even of a stone set up in rather late times to a person who fought valiantly in a battle but emerged unscathed.

None of the hero-stones bears any sculpture which could be termed a portrait: the sculptor's aim has been to picture the valourous deeds of the hero or his journey from the field of battle to the hero's heaven. The inscription was at least as important as the sculpture. We are told that the sculptors were rewarded handsomely for their work and that a king of great prowess set up a stone in memory of 'Our Lady of Chastity' such stones must indeed have been carved into good likenesses. The principal aim, however, was not portraiture. The reason is obvious. The testimony of the Tamil classics to the offering of worship to hero-stones is wanting neither in perspicacity nor in conclusiveness. On the numerous memorial stones we come across in south India we have it set out, with all the authenticity of contemporary and solemn records, that worship was offered to them and that grants of land were made to support the services, even though the memorials were raised to a woman famous only because she gave up her life to prove her constancy to her husband or to a warrior undistinguished except by his valour. Nowhere do we have a hint that the sculptures were intended to serve for portraits. The sculptures on a memorial stone blazon the exploits of the hero and immortalize the scenes in which he won himself endless fame, but they do not seek to portray his figure or features. The sculptures were superfluous adornment and portraiture was not attempted. These stones,— with the obvious exception of stones set up to beasts or of those installed in memory of brave warriors who did not lose their lives in their valorous exploits, — were intended for worship,

　　　　　South Indian Portraits in Stone and Metal

and for that purpose it was by no means essential that they should have been fashioned into portraits. Further, it is also clear that worship was offered only to the stones installed in memory of deceased heroes. The conclusions are thus forced on us that the worship of a memorial stone was conditional on the death of the person in whose memory the stone was set up and that it was not essential that the stone should stand carved into a portrait of the deceased. The memorial stone must, therefore, belong to a class distinct from the stone statue.

It is occasionally suggested that stones were set up as memorials because of a dim feeling that they ought to be propitiated. Even though traces of the worship of menhirs are discernible in the cult of the hero-stone, we cannot be oblivious of the fact that even in the 'age of the Sangam,'— the earliest period of south Indian culture for which we have sufficient or cogent evidence,— the Tamils and the other related people of the south had outgrown that very primitive cult, and the psychology of the worship they offered to the hero-stone had undergone a sublimation which is beyond the mental range of the devotee of the mere menhir. The menhir must be an unworked piece of stone: it cannot be a wrought stone, nor can it be of metal: so, when statues of stone, worked not only into the human shape but also into likenesses of the persons whose memory was sought to be preserved, came into vogue and, later, when statuettes of metal came to be installed, whether in addition to or in substitution of stone-sculptures, the obliteration of the menhir-cult must have been complete.

VI

MEMORIAL TEMPLES

It cannot be denied that a statue may be worshipped on the death of its subject, and it is also indisputable that many of the statues to which worship was offered were located in temples. These facts may be at the bottom of the popular belief that certain temples are sepulchral in origin.

A very common conviction in the Tamil country is that some temples to Siva have been raised on the spots where human beings had been interred on their death. The evidence relied on in support of the belief are the traditions that some famous *siddhas* (adepts) lie buried in certain temples in the Tamil country[24] and that saints and teachers other than *siddhas*

---

24. My friend, Pandit S. Somasundara-Desikar, has kindly sent me a copy of a stray Tamil verse which seems to give the names of the respective temples in the outer courts of which lie buried the eighteen *Siddhas* (seers) famous in Tamil literature:
Tiru-Mular at Tillai
Rama-deva at Alagar-malai
Kumbha-muni at Anantasayanam
Idaik-kadar at Tiruv-arunai
Dhanvantri at Vaithisvarankoyil
Valmiki at Ettukudi

are interred in some other temples,—for instance, Panini and Pattanattu-Pillai at Tiruvorriyur, and Sadasiva-Brahmam at Nerur. The occurrence of terms such as *pali*[25] and (*mayanam*[26] in the names of certain ancient temples to Siva in the Tamil land suggests that those temples might have been built in cremation-grounds,— a suggestion by no means inappropriate in view of some aspects of the cult of Siva.

Professed historians too seem to believe that they have come across satisfactory evidence of the sepulchral character of some Siva temples. It has been claimed that 'epigraphical

Kamala-muni at 'Arur among the Balla-sayana'
Bhoga-natha at Palni
Matsya-muni at Tirupparankunram
Konkana at Tirupati
Patanjali at Ramesvaram
Nandi-deva at Shiyali
Bodha-guru at Setupati
Pampatti at Sankarankoyil
Sattai-muni at Jyoti-rangam
Suadara-Ananda-deva at Madura
Kudambar at Mayavaram
Goraksha at Poyyut
Karuvur-devar, another well-known *siddha*, is buried in the circuit of the temple at Karur.

25.   A well-known temple goes by the name of Tiru-aradai-perum- pah. In Tamil characters the word *pali is chk* word[S3]. The word *paliya* in Gujarati means a memorial stone (*ASI. W. AR.*, 1906: 38: 15, 1907: 35: 33). Is the Gujarati word allied to the Tamil word and was it applied to places where memorial stones had been set up or memorial temples erected?

26.   This Tamil word [S4], is derived from Skt *smasana*. Two well-known temples go by names of which *mayanam* is a part, Tiruk-Kadavur-nayarm and Tiru-Nalurt-tiru- mayanain,

evidences as to Siva temples being actually erected on the very spot where important personages were buried are not wanting in south Indian inscriptions.'[27] This is a mere assertion and cannot carry conviction till the texts of the inscriptions are published. Let us, however, examine the instances on which the above statement has been or might be based.[28]

An inscription of the 9th century A.D. at Solapuram records that 'after Prithvi-Gangaraiyar had died, his son, the great Rajaditya caused to be built'... 'on the spot where his father had been laid abed' a 'temple of Isvara' and also a 'house to the dead.'[29] Clearly, two structures were built—the temple and the house to the dead,—and so they could not both have stood on the exact spot where Prithvi-Ganga had been 'laid abed': it is but reasonable to assume that it was the 'house to the dead' that was built over that exact spot. The temple could not, therefore, have been raised over the remains of Prithvi-Ganga. Perhaps the structure which has been taken to be a 'house to the dead' was no more than a platform,[30] and, perhaps no bones nor ashes were deposited in the spot where Prithvi-Ganga was laid abed. All that this inscription could be taken to show is that a structure,— perhaps no more than

---

27.   ASL S. AR., 1916: 34.

28.   See *MER.*, 1914: 107: 47.

29.   *EI* vii. 192-3. In this rendering, I have substituted 'laid abed' for 'buried', and 'house to the dead' for 'house for the deceased (*i.e.* tomb)'. The words Ir. the inscription, *palli paduttav-idattu* do not indubitably point to burial.

30.   The term which has been read as *atiyta-garamum* can with perhaps with equal fitness be read as *atiytakamum* and taken to be a *vulgarisation* of *adhityaka* and not of *atita-griha*.

                          South Indian Portraits in Stone and Metal

a platform— was raised over his last resting place. The term 'to lay abed' being commonly used where a dead person was laid to his last rest, whether in the lap of mother earth or on a funeral pyre, we cannot be sure whether his bones or ashes would have been deposited at the spot whereon the 'house to the dead' was built. We have therefore, to gather that the 'house to the dead' or a mere platform,— whichever it was— was built on the spot where the king died, or where his mortal remains were placed last for interment or cremation, and that the 'temple of Isvara' was built in immediate vicinity.

The stone-slab set up in memory of the Saiva teacher, Vidya-rasi (9th cent. A.D.), after his death shows him as a *linga*: probably it was set up in a prominent place in the temple of Dharmapuri: but there is no reason to believe that the slab was ever installed over his grave.

An inscription of 1513-4 A.D.[31] says that Sankara- guru of the Pasupata-Sambhava-diksha who 'attained Sivahood' on that date 'had become a *linga* through the great penance'[32] of his preceptor: this too is no more helpful than the others. It has been suggested that 'evidently like the present-day preceptors of the Lingayats in the Kanarese country, these teachers of the Pasupata-Saiva sect, were buried in the temple premises with a *linga* fixed over their tombs' and that 'in course of time these latter came to be worshipped in the same manner as the *lingas* which had no connection with tombs.'[33] It has to be noticed that though the shrine was known as 'Sankara-prasada' after

---

31.   48:1 At Peddakodamagundla.

32.   MER., 1914: 143 of 1913, and *Ib.*, 1914: 107: 47.

33.   *Ib.*, 1914: 107: 47.

the deceased, the *linga* itself did not bear his name. Further, the *linga* stood in a shrine of a temple dedicated to Uttaresvara; so, even if we are to assume that an idol must have been installed over the last remains of Sankara-guru, it could be only a *linga* in the shrine and not the idol known as Uttaresvara.

At Rayadurga, an inscription of 1612 A.D. is found on a slab stating that 'a chief' of the place 'granted a village for the worship of the *Isvara-sthana* of his mother,'[34] and it has been suggested that by the *Isvara-sthana* was 'evidently meant the shrine with *linga* built over her tomb.'[35] But there is no reason for assuming that there was a temple or that it was a tomb: the inscription was found on a slab of stone lying under the shade of a tree.

Let us now turn to a very interesting class of temples peculiar to the Tamil country and called *palli-padai* or *pallip-padai*.[36] Very few of them are known to us today, and our knowledge of them is due solely to the discovery of inscriptions in which they are mentioned.

At Tondamanad, where perhaps the Chola king Aditya I (c. 900 A.D.) died, a *palli-padai* temple was built to him and called Adityesvara after him.[37] Arim-jaya, a grandson of Aditya I, and king of the Chola line in the latter half of the tenth century A.D., having died at Arrur, his grandson, Rajaraja I, built years afterwards a temple in another village, Melpadi, and named it Arimjaya-isvara, after his deceased grandfather: this temple

34. *Ib.*, 1914: 112 of 1913.

35. *Ib.*, 1914: 107: 47.

36. In Tamil characters, the words are chk and Chk

37. 49[S5]:3. *MER.*, 1904: 230 of 1903 ; 1905: 42: 9; 1907: 71: 30; 1921; 95 26; *SIL*, iii. 22, 237-8 ; ASI. S. AR1916: 34.

too is stated to have been raised as a *palli-padai*.[38] At Palaiyaru, a place which the Chola kings made almost their Windsor, a *pallip-padai* temple was built in the name of Panchavan Madevi, a queen of Rajaraja I, in the time of his son, Rajendra I.[39] Another *palli-padai* temple must have given its name to a village near Chidambaram called Vikrama-sola-nallur, for it had two *aliases*, Akkan-pallip-padai,[40] and a shorter form, Pallip-padai.[41] Evidently, the village was named,—or renamed,—after Vikrama-Chola (1118-39 A.D.), and the *palli-padai* was built in the name of his *akkan* or elder sister. Somewhere in the vicinity of Tirunirmalai, there was a place called Palli-padai-agaram,[42] which must have owed its name to a *palli-padai* temple in it.

The term *palli-padai* is now forgotten and its significance has yet to be traced and fixed. As the verbal form, *palli-paduitu*, is often applied to the interring of the last remains of a person worthy of veneration, *palli-padai* would seem to refer to the place where the mortal remains of a man are laid. But what are we to understand when we are told that a temple was raised by way of a *palli-padai* to a person?

The inscriptions which mention *palli-padais* throw no light. The *palli-padais* of which we have any knowledge seem to have been raised by kings of the Chola dynasty and dedicated to Siva and they seem to have been constructed when the influence of preceptors of the Lakulisa sect was

---

38. *MER.*, 1921: 95: 26; *SIL*, iii. 22.

39. *MER.*, 1927: 76: 12.

40. *Ib.*, 1914: 275 of 1913.

41. *Ib* 1914: 276 of 1913.

42. *Ib.*, 1913; 559 of 1912.

predominant in the Chola court. On the evidence now before us it is impossible to say whether *palli-padai* temples were peculiar to the Cholas or to the Lakulisa sect or if they could be dedicated to gods other than Siva. The memorial temple which, as we have seen, was raised at Solapuram by Rajaditya in memory of his father Prithvi- Ganga at or adjacent to the spot where Prithvi-Ganga had been laid to rest may, possibly, be also a *palli-padai* temple, and might have been raised also under Lakulisa influence.[43]

One of the cantos of Kamban's famous Tamil version of the *Ramayana* is now known as *Palli-y-adai-padalam*. The title not being quite appropriate to the contents of the canto, the suggestion has been made by an eminent scholar[44] that the correct reading of the title of the canto is *Palli-padai-padalam*, for the canto deals with the incidents relating to the cremation of the corpse of Dasaratha. Two circumstances are significant: the canto refers to the cremation, not the interment, of the corpse, and it makes no mention of a memorial having been raised at the place of cremation or elsewhere,— much less of a statue being placed in the memorial. We may therefore, infer that Kamban held that the term *palli-padai* was not inappropriate to instances where the corpse was disposed of by cremation and no memorial was raised in honour of the deceased, whether in the

---

43. Certain important developments in the religious history of south India might have been due to some of these practices. This is not the place where the subject could be gone into at length. I have dealt with it in my forthcoming books, *Saivism in South India: the Mediaeval Period,* and *The Evolution of the Temple.*

44. Pandit M. Raghava-Aiyangar, in the course of a kind conversation with me. He assures me that his suggestion is supported by the readings he found in some reliable manuscripts.

                    South Indian Portraits in Stone and Metal

form of a statue or a temple or of both. If this is the meaning of a *palli-padai*, it must follow that when a temple is raised as a *palli-padai* in honour of a deceased person it is not essential that his corpse or ashes should be deposited underneath it nor that a statue of him should be placed in it.

The inscription which mentions that Rajaraja I built a temple as a *palli-padai* to his grandfather, Arimjaya makes it clear that the temple was built not only years after Arimjaya's death but also at a place different from the one where he had breathed his last. Neither the bones nor the ashes are likely to have been preserved till Rajaraja chose years afterwards, to build the temple, and much less is Rajaraja likely to have disturbed and shifted them from Arrur to Melpadi. This instance makes it obvious that a *palli-padai* temple was not necessarily one raised of the spot where were buried the last remains of the person in whose memory the temple was built.

It follows that a *palli-padai* must be a temple built in honour of a deceased person, and perhaps named after him. We know of temples which were built by the persons after whom they were named, but they are not known to be *palli-padai* temples. The explanation must be that such temples were named after the respective builders, and not necessarily after their death and as memorials to them. The *palli-padai* temple must, therefore, be a shrine built not only in honour of a person but also in memory of him after his death.

The peculiar classes of primitive structures called dolmens and cromlechs are sometimes pointed to as forerunners of the memorial temple in south India. Structures of this type are not rare in south India, but they cannot be temples as they contain neither an idol nor sculptured figures for worship. Occasionally, we find in south India a structure open on one side formed of four slabs of stone,— three set up on end and the fourth laid on top as a covering,— in which a *linga* is set up in the middle. Sometimes, figures are carved on the slab facing the opening,—the figures being representations of a hero or heroes who fell in a raid and perhaps also of the hero's wife who became a *sati* on his death. The one notable feature of these structures is that they are erected generally on rocky surfaces and there are no traces whatever to show that the flooring was ever disturbed so that the bones or the ashes of the dead man might be buried underneath. So, we would be wrong if we sought to identify such structures with the earlier and cruder forms of the corridor-tomb. They are developments of either the hero-stone or the dolmen in deliberate imitation of the temple. They are memorials to the dead but they are by no means sepulchral shrines. Really, they are hero-shrines, the utmost that we can be sure of being that they were built on the spots where the persons to whom they were memorials had died or had been cremated,— such spots having been thought worthy of veneration. If so, some of those shrines might have been raised in crematoria, agreeably to the cult of Siva which associates him with cremation-grounds. Such shrines would not, however, be sepulchral. The temple which the Chera king, Sem-Kuttuvan, is said to have built in memory of the hero and the heroine of the *Silappadiharam*, though perhaps an edifice grand in proportions, finished in workmanship and imposing in appearance, must have been essentially a hero-shrine.

  South Indian Portraits in Stone and Metal

To be really sepulchral in character a temple must be built either over the corpse or over the ashes of a human being and must be dedicated to a *deity* and not to a mere man, however, highly he might be venerated. The essentials of a temple are an idol to which the temple is dedicated and a *sanctum sanctorum* in which the idol is housed. In the case of a truly sepulchral temple, one would expect the idol to be installed right' over the grave and the *sanctum sanctorum* to cover the idol and, therefore, the grave as well. If the grave lies outside the *sanctum sanctorum* we cannot be sure that the temple is really sepulchral, for, the burial might have taken place long after the building of the temple, or the grave might have become included in the temple owing to its expanding beyond its original limits.

The remains of the famous Vaishnava teacher, Ramanuja, are said to lie buried in one of the *prakaras* (circuits) of the great temple to Vishnu at Srirangam, and a shrine has been raised over the spot: it is even said that the image of that teacher has been placed right over the place where the corpse was interred. The shrine is in a *prakara* while the image of Vishnu to which the temple is dedicated stands about a furlong off in the principal temple. Any one who has been to the temple at Srirangam will admit that it is highly probable that the spot where Ramanuja was buried was originally beyond the pale of the temple and that owing to its expansion the spot fell within the confines of the temple as we see it today. The grave of Pattanattu-Pillai at Tiruvorriyur and that of Sadasiva-Brahmam at Nerur, for instance, are only in the outer circuits and are much posterior to the building of those temples. In the case of even the *siddhas* it is difficult to demonstrate that the grave of any of them is in the *sanctum sanctorum*, much less under the idol. The 'temple of Isvara' at Solapuram was obviously built at a spot different from the one where Prithvi-Ganga had been 'laid abed.' On his death, Sankara-guru, was buried in the temple of Uttaresvara, a *linga* was set up over the grave and a shrine known as 'Sankara- prasada' was raised over the *linga*: the idol of Uttaresvara stood neither in the shrine 'Sankara-prasada' nor over the grave of Sankara-guru. It is almost fantastic to suppose that the corpse of Arimjaya having been originally interred at Arrur where he died,—or his ashes having been first committed to the earth at Arrur,— the mouldered remains were many years later dug up and shifted to Melpadi by his grandson Rajaraja I and that over the new grave a sepulchral temple was raised. The hero-shrine of the *Silappadiharam* was not built in Madura where the hero had met with his tragic end nor at Tiruchengodu which was the place from which the heroine had mounted up to heaven but at Vanji, the capital of the Chera king.

Of the numerous sects of the Hindus there are some which usually bury their dead, and there are other sects with whom burial is an exception confined mainly to the interment of those who had been members of orders of renunciation. Among the sects which follow Vishnu, the practice is to raise a mound over the grave and grow on it some holy basil: the setting up of a statue over the grave is unknown, the case of Ramanuja being a unique exception. Among those sects which follow Siva the practice is to set up a *linga*. A son who revered his father or a disciple who venerated a preceptor installed a *linga* over the grave of the father or the preceptor and worshipped it: if he could afford it, he built even a rudimentary shrine over *linga* and grave. But a *linga* set up over

   South Indian Portraits in Stone and Metal

a grave lost greatly in status: from a symbol of the divine it degenerated into a sign of the deification of the human being who lay buried underneath. It suffered from its having been raised as a memorial to a mere man who, whatever his claims to the respect of his neighbours, could prefer no title to the signal honour of general worship. The natural result of such a *linga* losing its character as the symbol for the divine is that a very clear distinction grew up between temples in which the *linga* stood as the symbol of the divine and shrines in which it was a memorial to a man buried below. So, the temples of even such sects cannot be deemed to be sepulchral in origin.[45]

We are often told of finds of bones at the base of temples,[46] but no one has noted what the character of those temples was nor noted precisely whether the bones were found in the foundations or in the space enclosed by the walls of the foundations. These points are of real importance: if they were merely sepulchral shrines raised in the *prakaras* of temples, the discovery of bones would only confirm the character of the structure: and if the bones were discovered in the foundations

---

45. An inscription found in a temple at Chatsu in the Jaipur State says that the Guhilot king Baladitya, who reigned early in the 9th cent. A.D. (*EI.* xviii, 106, n. 3), erected a temple to Murari in commemoration of his queen Rattava who was then dead (*Ib* xii. 10-17). It will be noticed that this temple was merely commemorative, that there is no hint that it was sepulchral or that it had been raised near the spot where Rattava had breathed her last, and that the temple was dedicated to Vishnu. Probably this temple and the *palli-padai* temples belong to the same type.

46. I am free to admit that I have heard more than once of bones having been found below the *sanctum* (see also *ASI.* S.A.E., 1916: 34), but *I* am not satisfied that the facts were observed with precision.

they would establish only the prevalence in south India of the practice, which, has obtained all over the wide world, of offering human-sacrifices when laying the foundation- stones of large and costly buildings.

Perhaps the belief about some temples being mausoleums might never have come into vogue had the distinction between a temple to a deity and a shrine to a man been clearly borne in mind. Is Westminster Abbey a sepulchral church in the true sense for the reason that the most illustrious of Englishmen are buried within its wells?

For the discussion in which we are engaged it seems to matter little whether the temple was dedicated to Vishnu or Siva, and still less whether the temple or the grave was prior in point of time, and perhaps even less whether the idol was or was not in the form of a *linga* or whether what was interred was the corpse or the ashes left over after cremation. The point of real importance is whether we are concerned with a temple raised to a deity or with a shrine in which a man is worshipped. If this distinction is kept steadily in mind, it is not easy to point even to one instance of a temple to a deity which is really a mausoleum.

Having reached this conclusion it is unnecessary to investigate whether an idol set up to a deity in a temple might be a portrait of any human being such as the builder of the temple. But, in view of a curious practice which seems to have obtained in Java in early times, it is desirable that we should examine whether the practice is traceable in south India which was the most fruitful source of much of the higher culture of Java for some centuries.

                South Indian Portraits in Stone and Metal

'From the old Javanese chronicles we learn that when a king had died and his body had been cremated it was the custom to raise a temple over his ashes and to enshrine in it a divine image representing a certain god, usually a Buddha or Siva, but with the deceased king's features. The monarch, divine in origin and essence, had become re-absorbed into the deity from which he sprang. Of course, the conception of the king as a divine being is by no means exclusively Javanese. It belongs to the Orient in general and it is well-known that when Greek civilization had conquered the Near East and in their turn Eastern ideas pervaded the West, one of them was the divinity of the king. In India, too, the idea prevailed, it being set forth at some length in the well-known *Law Book of Manu* (vii. 3-11), On the Indian continent, however, the conception of kings as divine beings does not appear to have led to a custom of showing them in the semblance of gods such as we find in Java.'[47]

No evidence of this practice is to be found in India. Literary evidence seems to be totally lacking. Only three inscriptions, all of which come from the Kanarese country, appear to evidence the prevalence of practices analogous to the Javanese custom: but a close examination reveals that the evidence is far from satisfactory.

An inscription at Kurgod describes, with considerable imagery, how, when the Sinda king Rachamalla I, of the 32th century A.D., 'was brilliantly advancing in the course of his reign, the god (Siva) one day appeared in revelation' accompanied by his attendants, 'and king Rachamalla

---

47. Prof. J. Ph. Vogel, on pp. 80-1 of *The Influences of Indian Art*, by **Strzygowski and others (The India Society).**

reverently gazing and offering salutation, clasped his hands in worship, and Hara (Siva) smiling, held out the hand of security, to the end that he should behold Kailasa; and (the king). . . having. . . performed worship of Siva. . . established for his descendants prosperity of rule (in bearing) the burden of earth, being while still in the body ... (and) even after attaining a place in the world of Siva, he formed a *linga* for the earth by union therewith.' The inscription proceeds: 'so having come and stood at the western side of (the temple of) the god Svayambhu of Kurugodu, and arisen in the form of a *linga* he became very famous under the title of 'the God Udbhava-Rachamallesvara.'[48]

On a casual perusal the inscription would appear to suggest that on his death Rachamalla sought to maintain contact with the earth, that he, therefore, came down to the temple of Kurugodu and stationed himself beside the god Svayambhu of that temple, that henceforward he was treated as a god and that the name of that god was, Rachamalla.

This interpretation would imply that in his descent to earth Rachamalla retained his old shape and his old name, the only difference being that in his descent he had become transformed into a god with a body fashioned of stone or metal instead of the ancient flesh and blood. The image of Rachamalla would then have been a perfect portrait indeed and the Javanese practice would have had its echo at Kurugodu. But the inscription itself contains a statement which refutes these fanciful speculations. In the attempt to maintain contact with the earth, Rachamalla got transformed into a *linga*, and it is

---

48.   *EI*, xvi. 278-9, 282-3.

                              South Indian Portraits in Stone and Metal

in the form of a *linga* that the god Rachamalla arose from the earth. Once a *linga*, never a portrait statue. So, the inscription, stripped of the embellishments, says nothing more than that on Rachamalla's death a *linga* was set up in a shrine to the west of the main shrine dedicated to god Svayambhu and that the *linga* was named after Rachamalla.

An inscription at Asandi, dated 1191 A.D., states that 'on Bammarasa-deva and his mother Ganga-Mahadevi, departing to *svarga* having performed the funeral ceremonies, he sent to Sri-parvata and fetching from the Patala-Ganga the ornamental *linga* stones found there, set them up, under the name of the gods Brahmesvara and Gangesvara.'[49] [S1]Were Bammarasa and Ganga-devi set up as gods, and, if they were, did they retain their human shape? The latter question is answered by the statement in the inscription itself that *lingas* of stone were set up, and the answer to the former question is that the idols were consecrated in their respective names. No question of portraiture arises at all.

An inscription at Harihar, dated 1280 A.D., states that the village of Harihar was freed from taxes by Mahadeva (1260-71 A.D.), a king of the Yadava line, during a victorious expedition, that some years after Mahadeva's death, Saluva-Tikkama, who had been Mahadeva's general and continued to hold that office under Mahadeva's nephew and successor, happening to pass by Harihar, recollected how Mahadeva had made it free of taxes and that he resolved forthwith that the memory of Mahadeva should be perpetuated in that place. The inscription proceeds thus: 'Saluva-Tikkama, begging

---

49.   *EC.* 6Kd;Kdl57.

permission to make a temple in this Harihara-pura in the name of his master, Mahadeva, carried out his intention in the following manner:—As, in order to show to mortals that the god will bestow benefits on his worshipers, he had made the (place) *manya* (tax-free), Isvara directed Tikkama saying that Mahadeva must ever remain in this my city having obtained divinity.—(Therefore), near to the god who thus directed his mind, he set up his lord Mahadeva in the form of (*or*, by means of the image of) Lakshmi-Narayana.'[50]

If literally interpreted, the passage stating that Saluva-Tikkama 'set up his lord in the form' of the god would have its parallel in the verses of *Genesis*: 'And God said, Let us make man in our image, after our likeness,' and 'So God created man in his own image, in the image of God created he him.'[51] Such an interpretation, however, is impossible, for

---

50. *EC*. 11 Dg: Dg 59. At the end of this extract, I have substituted the words 'he set up his lord Mahadeva in the form of (or by means of the image of) Lakshmi-Narayana' for the words of the original translation, 'he set up his master Mahadeva in the image of (the god) Lakshmi-Narayana.' I have done so on the authority of the eminent scholar, Rao Bahadur R. Narasimhacharya, whom I consulted on this important and difficult inscription Mr. Narasimbacharya's opinion, deserves to be set down here: 'There is no question of any portrait here. Mr Rice's translation, "in the image of" has caused this unnecessary confusion.
     When a *linga* is set up, the suffix *Isvara* is added to the name of the man who sets it up; *e.g.*, Raja-raja-Isvara, Bucha- Isvara, and so forth. Similarly, the name of the Vishnu image, Lakshmi-Narayana m this case, is added to the name of the setter-up and the image set up is styled Mahadeva-Lakshmi-Narayana. It means merely that an image of Lakshmi-Narayana was set up in honour of Mahadeva.'

51. *Genesis*, l. 26, 27.

the Lord Mahadeva was dead long ago and 'the Lord' could no longer be set up in the form of the god,— even if that was practicable. Nor can we justly infer that the image of the god was carved into a resemblance of the king, for the inscription says not that the god was set up 'in the form' of the king but that the king was set up 'in the form' of the god. The plain purport of the inscription, therefore, is that some years after the death of king Mahadeva his general set up an image of Vishnu (Lakshmi-Narayana) beside the image of Siva and that the new image was consecrated in memory of Mahadeva.

An inscription of about 1363 A.D. at Korukonda says that the local chieftain's Vaishnava preceptor, Bhattari, 'told the chief one day that he had reached the last of his human births and as soon as the mortal frame was given up he would appear in the form of Lakshmi-Narasimha on the hill at Korukonda.' The preceptor died some time afterwards and his words were promptly forgotten by the chief. But the preceptor appeared in a dream to a dancing-girl and assured her that he had manifested himself on the Parasara hill at Korukonda. Thereupon, the dancing-girl went about begging and in 1863 A.D. built a temple on the hill and consecrated it to Parasara-Narasimha, and, perhaps with the help of the chieftain, presented two villages 'for the maintenance of worship and offerings.'[52]

Bhattari's assurance that he would appear in the form of Laksmi-Narasimha may raise a doubt whether the image of Lakshmi-Narasimha was fashioned into a likeness of Bhattari. But the doubt is possible only if the idol set up as Lakshmi-Narasimha could be taken as a transformation of Bhattari or

---

52.   *MER.*, 1912: 87-8: 68

at least as a symbol of Bhattari's spirit, but nowhere in the tenets of Vaishnavism do we find the slightest support for either of the hypotheses. Bhattari's words can mean no more than that his memory would be commemorated by an idol dedicated to Lakshmi-Narasimha and by a temple raised to it.

The idol installed by Saluva-Tikkama in memory of king Mahadeva was not even named after the king, nor was the idol set up by the dancing-girl named after Bhattari: being images of Vishnu they would have been figures of human shape and not *lingas*, but there are no indications whatever that they were modelled in the likeness of King Mahadeva or of Bhattari. The *linga* stone installed in memory of queen Ganga-devi was named Gangesvara and not Gangesvari: So, Ganga-devi when represented by a *linga* became Gangesvara, suffering even a change of sex. Portraiture is thus evidently out of question.

Obviously we have no ground whatever for assuming that an idol set up in memory of a deceased person might have been carved into an image of him nor for believing that any of the idols were located over graves.

                    South Indian Portraits in Stone and Metal

VII

STATUES TO ANCESTORS

Traces are now discernible of an ancient Indian custom of setting up statues in the likeness of deceased persons which, however, is entirely different in character from the Javanese practice.

Our knowledge of this class of statues is due to the recent discovery of Bhasa's play, *Pratima-Nataka*, or *The Statues*.

No Indian story is better known than that of Rama, the hero of the *Ramayana* Rama was sent into exile by his father Dasaratha, king of Ayodhya, at the instance of Kaikeyi,—a step-mother,—whose object was thereby to secure the throne for her own son, Bharata. Dasaratha, overwhelmed with the grief of separation from Rama, died almost immediately afterwards of a broken heart. The circumstance that Bharata was not in Ayodhya when Rama went into exile and Dasaratha breathed his last is taken up by Bhasa and turned to unique dramatic purpose.

Bharata and the courier who had been sent to fetch him journey post-haste,—the messenger having tactfully represented that Dasaratha was seriously ill. When Bharata reaches the outskirts of Ayodhya he is asked to tarry just a while outside the city limits to allow the inauspicious influence of *Krittika* to pass by. Espying in the vicinity a temple which is visible through the trees, he goes to it for rest and worship. The temple had just been whitewashed and cleared of dove-cots and been garnished with wreaths and festoons; flowers and fried rice had been sprinkled on the floor and sand had been spread along the walks,— all in expectation of a visit to be paid by the queens of Dasaratha. Bharata, ignorant of the character of the temple and the cause of these preparations, fancies it to be some festive day and walks up to the temple, but he finds no symbols distinctive of one of other of the deities to whom temples are reared. Walking in, he finds four statues of exquisite workmanship,— a cluster of four deities, so to say,— but having no means of discovering whom they represented, he finds it impossible to choose the appropriate form of salutation. Just then, the keeper of the temple enters and finds a stranger,—Bharata being unknown to him,— who, he notes, looks but little different from the statues. Bharata is about to bow down to the statues when the keeper suspecting that he might be a Brahmana, asks him to desist as the statues were representations, not of gods, but only of Kshatriyas. On the keeper giving the further information that they were Ikshvaku kings, Bharata feels elated at having accidentally obtained the great privilege of paying his respects to his ancestors. Questioning the keeper further, he learns that the first three statues represent, respectively, Dilipa, Raghu and Aja, kings of the Ikshvaku dynasty. Knowing as Bharata does that his father Dasaratha was son of Aja, grandson of Raghu and great-grandson of Dilipa, and finding the statues

                 South Indian Portraits in Stone and Metal

arranged in the order of descent, he has no difficulty in inferring that the fourth statue must represent the fourth king of the dynasty, Dasaratha.[53] But he remembers that the first three kings were no longer in the land of the living: if the first three were dead, as they certainly were, what of the fourth? To this question, Bharata could frame no answer in his own mind,— so quickly do suspicions, doubts and apprehensions intrude themselves,—and so unwilling is he to accept Dasaratha for dead. Unable to bear the suspense, he puts the very significant question, 'Are statues set up to kings when yet they are alive'? He gets an emphatic 'No' for reply. This is, indeed, an abrupt disclosure to him of Dasaratha's death, and he stands staggered. The keeper, ignorant that the person to whom he is talking is Bharata, adds a touch or two which, in a flash, reveal to Bharata how his mother had been the ignoble cause of his father's death. Unable to bear this double load of disaster and disgrace, Bharata falls in a swoon, and the keeper of the *devakula*, who had been growing suspicious, obtains confirmation that the person before him is Bharata. The queens coming just then on the scene, a chamberlain tells them that that building, which surpasses even palaces in height, is the statue-house of Dasaratha, and he adds regretfully that the mighty Dasaratha having become mere stone, people may pass by and in and out, without let or hindrance, and not even join their hands in salutation. His eyes then fall upon the prostrate figure of the youth whose close resemblance to the dead king strikes him at once. The keeper reveals to the chamberlain that the prostrate figure is none other than Bharata. On Bharata reviving and attempting

---

53.   This is the genealogy which Bhasa deliberately adopts.

to speak the chamber lain is so struck by the resemblance of the voice to that of Dasaratha that he doubts whether that king's statue had started speaking. Bharata having fully recovered, a painful scene follows in which he upbraids his mother with having been so covetous of the kingdom for him that she had recked not if in consequence Rama went into exile and Dasaratha died, and he announces his resolve to follow his exiled brother,— for, to him there is Ayodhya where Rama tarries.[54]

This scene makes it obvious that though Bharata was not aware of statue-houses and of statues in them, all the other characters were quite well acquainted with them. Statues were installed only for those who were dead and were ranged in the order of descent. That the statues were exceedingly faithful as portraits is brought out by such slight but significant touches as where the temple-keeper and the palace chamberlain are made to recognise the resemblance which Bharata bore to the statues. The sculptors must have been capable of bringing out the expression which must have been common to all the four members of the Ikshvaku line,— for the keeper of the statue-house found Bharata but little different from the statues,— and at the same time to reproduce the individual features of each of the four kings. The statue-house was evidently a towering structure and was located, perhaps, in a grove but, certainly, outside the limits of the capital. Temples were quite common in those days and they bore distinctive symbols showing to

---

54. In this account I have adopted some of the language of Mr. K. Pisharoti's translation of this play. His version of this Act, together with some notes and comment by him, will be found in *QJMS*. xii. 375-96.

　　　　South Indian Portraits in Stone and Metal

which deity they had been reared, but statue-houses bore no such symbols. Statue-houses were probably open on one side and had no doors. Even wayfarers could go in so freely and unceremoniously that the chamberlain feels that to Dasaratha turned to stone there might be none so poor to do reverence.

The keeper thought it worthwhile warning Bharata not to offer obeisance to the statues as he suspected that Bharata had taken them for gods, but, later, Bharata did pay obeisance to them when he was told that they were statues of his ancestors. From the circumstance that even way-farers might pay them the courtesy of a salutation we may infer that they were objects of reverence. From the facts that no priest seems to have been in attendance and that neither Bharata nor the queens offered any worship we might infer that the statues were not worshipped as idols are, were it not that the dramatic incidents which crowd into this act afford very little opportunity either to Bharata or to the queens to indulge in any formal worship. Bhasa is too much of a dramatist to intrude on the audience what are inessentials in a play.

Perhaps after the statues had been set up, they did not attract much attention, and it is no wonder that while the other members of the royal family know of statue-houses, Bharata knows nothing of them. When we note how it is not because of Dasaratha's statue having been set up but because of the expected visit of the queens that the statue-house had been whitewashed and rid of dove-cots, we may infer that once a statue had been set up and visited by the members of the family, the statues and the statue-house were both ignored till another death took another statue to the statue-house.

The term *devakula*, often applied in this play to these statue-houses, may mean merely a temple, or may mean a temple for a cluster of statues; perhaps, the statues were all set up at one time, or the temple was intended for a group of statues, though they were not all installed together. But why should Bhasa mention only four statues,— even curtailing for the purpose the long and distinguished roll of Ikshvaku kings? That the stage could not have accommodated more than four statues might be a reason, and the necessity for making the scene effective by making it brief might be another. If so, why were as many as three of the immediate ancestors of Dasaratha represented in statues? Even after making allowance for the dramatic necessity of showing statues of more than one dead king to Bharata so that doubts might be kindled in him about Dasaratha being dead, we cannot overlook the significance of the number three.

South Indian Portraits in Stone and Metal

VIII

ORIGINS

What may the origins of portraiture be in the south of India? No answer can be correct or comprehensive till we have studied all the various types of portraiture, but, unfortunately, the specimens that have come to our knowledge are almost all religious, in one sense or another. When a pilgrim is shown treading the weary path to a distant sanctuary or a devotee is portrayed in the temple or in the *stupa* which he erected or when for the benefit of his soul his image is placed in the attitude of worship or of service in the presence of an enshrined deity, or a figure of him is set up on the battlefield whereon he fell fighting the enemies of his liege-lord and he is offered worship because he has graduated into a godling, or an idol in his image is installed in a shrine built to honour him as the head of a sect, we have the religious instinct seeking vent in portraiture. The almost total absence of examples of sculptural portraiture fashioned from other motives is an obstacle to the elucidation of the fundamental ideas that impelled the artist to fashion portraits.

Occasionally we come across an example of a statue which had no religious purpose to fulfil or was not inspired by any feeling of a religious character. The iron statue in which Bhima was represented and the golden statue with which, according to a Tamil poem, the wrath of an offended king, Nannan, was sought to be appeased are obvious examples of portrait sculptures not inspired by religious motives, but the examples being neither numerous nor varied and the references to them being neither adequate nor explicit, we have not material enough on which to base a fairly comprehensive theory of the origin or the evolution of portrait sculpture.

The sculptures with which no religious motive can be associated seem to have been products of the instinct for art for art's sake. Such portraits were not worshipped. Those portraits which were set up from a religious motive were either worshipped at once or were eligible for worship in due course. The statuette of a devotee installed in a temple will be worshipped on behalf of his descendants from the time it is set up if it happens that the devotee was then dead: it will not be worshipped while he is alive, but on his death it would become eligible for worship. The distinction between the statues which might be called decorative and those which might be termed religious would, therefore, correspond to the distinction between the class of statues which were not worshipped and that of statues which were worshipped were it not that in the category of statues worshipped would fall those statues which were set up to devotees who were then alive. The sculptures which were worshipped were either rudimentary carvings in which no attempt at portraiture was ordinarily made or were statues or statuettes or relievos on which the sculptor had

   South Indian Portraits in Stone and Metal

bestowed skill enough to endow them with at least a passable likeness to the persons sought to be represented. Hero-stones belong to the class of rudimentary sculptures to which worship was offered, though occasionally a hero-stone might happen to be an excellent product of the sculptor's chisel.

The ceremonies with which hero-stones were installed and the ritual of the worship which was paid to them are closely akin to the funeral practices of those who came to the south of India from the north,— a circumstance which is confirmed by the hints which we obtain from the earliest surviving vestiges of Tamil literature which, in fact, is the earliest body of Dravidian literature now extant.[55] The popularity of the creed of the Buddha which the figures of the devotees in the Amaravati ruins speak to and the splendid Sanskrit verses which record the setting up of Mahendravarman's statue in the Trichinopoly rock-cut temple show beyond doubt that the earliest examples of portraiture in the south of India bear palpable traces of the culture of the north. Both the literary and the sculptural evidences, therefore, establish unambiguously that even in the earliest days of which we can now catch glimpses there was not much difference between the north and the south in respect of the ideas which influenced the evolution of portrait-sculpture. We have no reason, therefore, to assume that the motives which induced the south Indian to set up hero-stones or portrait sculptures were peculiar to him.

---

55. For some instances, see my *Portrait Sculpture in South India*, Chap V. For instances showing identity of the funeral ceremonies, see, in addition, *Aha-Nanuru*, 181, and *Pura-Nanuru*, 93, 231, 234, 240, 249, 860, 363.

We have already seen that the hero-stone has developed in south India on lines which the menhir did not take in other parts of the world. Was any other influence at work which diverted the course of development?

The *Satapatha Brahmana* and some other early scriptures of the Aryans of India mention an interesting rite,— the raising of a memorial to the dead. 'This is to be done a long time after the death; when even the year is forgotten is a suitable time. The bones are gathered from the hole in the earth or from the tree roots, in which case a verse is used which rather points to the ideas of real burial, and may suggest that once the gathering of the bones and the putting away of them in a relic mound were done when the body had decayed after normal burial. If the bones cannot be found,' another rite 'takes place: a garment is spread on the water's edge: the dead is called by name, and any beast that alights is treated as representing the bones: in the alternative, dust from the place is used. The night is spent in ceremonies: women beating their thighs with the right hand, with hair loosened, wailing, thrice in the course of the night dance thrice round the bones. Lutes are played, and— doubtless to scare away spirits— a noise made by the beating of an old shoe on an empty pot or in other ways. In the morning, the bones are taken to the new place of rest, which must be out of sight from the village, in a place where there is abundance of plants, around whose roots the fathers are said to creep, but no thorns. A hole is made or furrow is ploughed: seeds of all sorts are sowed and the bones deposited. The hole is then covered over with stones and earth to make a memorial mound: in it seeds are sown

     South Indian Portraits in Stone and Metal

to feed the dead, and pits are dug in it into which water and milk are poured to please the dead.'[56] occasionally, a pillar seems to have been set up on the mound. In the *Rig Veda* is to be found a hymn:[57]

Heave thyself, Earth, nor press thee downward heavily: afford him easy access, gently tending him. Cover him, as a mother wraps her skirt about her child, O Earth. Now, let the heaving earth be free from motion: yea, let a thousand clods remain above him. Be they to him a house distilling fatness, here let them ever be his place of refuge. I stay the earth from thee, while over thee I place this piece of earth. May I be free from injury. Here let the fathers keep this pillar (*sthuna* of the funeral monument) firm for thee, and there let Yama make for these an abiding place.

The stones of which mention is made above are sepulchral, set up as they were over the bones or the ashes of the deceased person, but hero-stones are not known to be at all sepulchral. Further, the funeral practices detailed above were appropriate to the funeral of any person, hero or coward, and could have had no connection with the cult of the hero. The rituals mentioned above seem to have been undergoing changes: the bones of the deceased were gathered for burial in a mound, and if they were not available the bones of birds were substituted; sometimes, the dust scraped from the spot of burial or cremation was considered enough. These rituals developed probably along other lines; the mound, for instance,

---

56.   Prof. A B. Keith, The Religion and the Philosophy of the Vedas and Upanishads, 421-2.

57.   *Rig-Veda*, x. 18, 11-3, quoted by P. T. Srinivasa-Aiyangar in his *Life in Ancient India in the Age of the Mantras*, 99.

developed into the *stupa* and the *sthuna* developed probably into the *tee* of the *stupa*. But it may still be that the cult of the hero- stone was to some extent affected by these practices, in so far at any rate as it allowed the hero-stone to be set up, in many instances, on the spot where the hero fell in battle or was cremated. Perhaps the memorial temple of south India too did not escape the influence of these practices.

The *Satapatha Brahmana*, for instance, requires that, in building the fire-altar for one of the sacrifices, a lotus-leaf and, on it, a golden plate, and, on that again, a golden image of a man (a *hiranyapurusha*)should be placed in the centre of the site chosen for the altar and it identifies the *hiranyapurusha* with the sacrifices himself.[58] The use in sacrifices of a figure in human shape is therefore, quite an ancient and sacrificed one and the identification of the golden figure with the sacrificer is not unlikely to have led to the development of portraiture in metal. Here perhaps is warrant enough for holding that portraiture in metal was not a much younger art than portraiture in stone. How far such practices might have led to the growth of the popular belief that temples are sepulchral is also a moot point on which we cannot easily express on opinion.

The sculptures which were carved into portraits were eligible for worship immediately or would become eligible in due course. The statues set up on the death of the subjects of portraiture were either memorial or sepulchral,— the sculptures in the latter case being installed over the spots where the bones or the ashes of the deceased persons had been interred. The eligibility of the statues for worship did not depend on whether they were memorial or were sepulchral.

---

58.   VII. 4. I, and Eggeling's note on p. 43 of his edn. in *SBE*.

                    South Indian Portraits in Stone and Metal

In Hindu ritual, worship is of many grades and kinds. The worship of an elder or a father who is alive is only an exaggerated mode of showing respect, and it differs essentially from the worship offered to the elder or the father when he has departed this life; the worship of the *manes* of the dead differs fundamentally from the worship of the godlings, whose worship in turn differs from the worship of God. What is worshipped by one person may not be worshipped by another: the spirit of a deceased person, for instance, is worshipped only by his descendant, and not by the members of a different family, nor even by the seniors in his own line. The ritual too varies with the nature of the worship. So, the term 'worship', frequently used in these pages, must be interpreted differently to suit the circumstances of the case.

What is the motive behind the memorial statue? For an answer we cannot do better than discover the purpose of the statues of which Bhasa has made excellent dramatic use.

We have already seen that Bhasa must have had a purpose in curtailing the number of Dasaratha's ancestors to three in the scene in which Bharata learns of Dasaratha's death. That is not the only scene in the play where Bhasa speaks of only four generations. We may go to an earlier scene: when Rama has left for the forest, and Dasaratha, overborne with grief, lies dying, Bhasa makes Dasaratha see his three immediate ancestors, Dilipa, Raghu and Aja, in a vision, and makes him ask them why when the time for his dwelling with them in their world had come they should have advanced to meet him and he assures them that he is going to them that he may join them. Further, Bhasa puts into Dasaratha's mouth a farewell to Rama, Sita and Lakshmana and an intimation that he was going thence to the side of his fathers. In a later scene, where, after Dasaratha's death Bharata goes to the forest in the hope of bringing Rama back from exile, Bhasa makes Sumantra introduce Bharata as the fourth from Raghu, the third from Aja and the second from Dasaratha. So, in telling out the tale of Rama's ancestors, when Dasaratha had himself become enrolled among the fathers, Sumantra omits Dilipa from the roll of the fathers, The mention of Dilipa, Raghu and Aja as the three ancestors of Dasaratha while Dasaratha was still alive, Dasaratha's assurance that he was going to the side of the fathers, the presence of those three fathers in his feverish fancy, if not actually on the stage, are very significant, but even more significant are the dropping out of Dilipa on Dasaratha's death, and the inclusion of Dasaratha among the fathers when Bharata reached Rama's camp months after the death of Dasaratha. The exigencies of the stage could not have dictated the omission of Dilipa when Sumantra counted out the ancestors of Bharata: the ancestors were not being marshalled then on the stage of the theatre. A definite purpose,— by no means dramatic,— has to be inferred from such deliberate inclusion and elimination.

The statue of Dasaratha in the *devakula* must have been installed within a few days of his death, for Bharata finds it in place when he hastens to Ayodhya. Dasaratha could not by then have become a *pitri*, but he stood beside Dilipa, Raghu and Aja who were his three immediate ancestors, that is, were his *pitris*. At the end of a year, on the performance of the *Sa-pindi-karana* ceremony, Dasaratha himself becomes a *pitri*.

          South Indian Portraits in Stone and Metal

Is it this process that was symbolised by the setting up of a statue to Dasaratha beside those of his three immediate ancestors? Does Bhasa's *devakula* serve for an ocular demonstration of the process of *Sa-pindi-karana*? On no other basis is it possible to explain the insistent reference of Bhasa to the three, immediate ancestors.

On the base of one of the Kushan statues discovered at Mathura runs an inscription which mentions a *devakula*, a garden and a tank. The actual discovery of a tank and the ruins of a temple within some yards of where the fragments of the statues lay strewn at Mathura has naturally led to the quite probable surmise that in the reign of the king of the statue of this inscription a *devakula* was constructed— or at least reconditioned,— a tank excavated near the *devakula* and a garden reared round it. When we note that the statue-house of the *Pratima Nataka* is called also a *devakula* and that Bharata espies it in a densely wooded grove, and that the Indian practice is to dig tanks in close vicinity to temples for the convenience of worshippers, we cannot but conclude that the statue-house of the *Pratima Nataka* has its replica in the Kushan *devakula* at Mathura.

If the statues claimed to be representations of Sisunaga kings are accepted as portraits of continuous descendants of the same royal line and if we admit the possibility of the statues having at one time stood under the same roof, we would have a gallery of statues which numbered four and represented four uninterrupted generations of one dynasty. If we may accept the identification of the various sculptures found along with the Kanishka statue at Mathura, we would have a *devakula* in which statues, of three generations of the Kushans were represented in the persons of Wema Kadphises, Kanishka and Kanishka's son. The statue of Chashtana would then form a fourth, but we are not able to relate it with precision to the group owing to our ignorance of Chastanas connection with the Kushans. The facts, however, would remain that in the same *devakula* there stood no more than four statues, that all of them,— at any rate, three— represented members of the same dynasty and that three of them were related as son, father and grandfather. The Sisunaga and the Kushan groups,— if they are really groups of the same family,— would appear to be replicas of the Ikshvaku group of Bhasa's play.

That the Ikshvaku *devakula* is paralleled in the Kushan *devakula* has been denied and it has been suggested that the Pallava portrait-group at Mahabalipuram could have served as a model to whosoever wrote the *Pratima Nataka*.[59][S2] If this view is to be accepted, the similarities pointed out above between the two *devakulas* must be ignored and we shall have to forget altogether that the statues of Simhavishnu and Mahendravarman I are the products of a different *motif* altogether. The two Pallavas are shown as builders of the temple in which they are figured, and not as *devas* set up in a *devakula*, but the *pratimas* of Bhasa are memorial statues standing for men being turned or already turned into *devas*. For the same reason the portrait-galleries at

Madura and other places are wholly unacceptable as parallels to the *devakula* of Bhasa. Indeed, we have not so far come across, in south India, any replica of the *devakula* of Bhasa.

---

59.   Dr. Hirananda-Sastri, Bhasa (ASI. 28), 26.

                    South Indian Portraits in Stone and Metal

Hindu observances, especially the funeral ceremonies, are largely symbolic. Brahmanism requires food to be offered to the *pitris*, and, in the earliest times, the *pitris* were imagined to be almost concretely, if not corporeally, present to eat the food. Could the fancy be more forcefully expressed than in this hymn of the *Rig Veda?*[60]

May the soma-loving fathers, who are both of low degree and of high rank, rise and accept the clarified butter we offer unto them they have come to us to preserve us from harm.

Salutation to the fathers, who were born before me, and those who, though born after me, have already departed from this world before me. Salutation to my fathers, who are sitting on the bare ground among friends well able to entertain them with the richest viands. My ancestors have honoured me with their presence. My fathers are sitting upon the *kusa* grass I have spread for them, and are eating the food, and drinking the soma juice I have placed before them.

Fathers, who are now sitting upon the *kusa* grass, you will have to protect us, your children, ignorant of the ways of the world. Accept this clarified butter we have prepared for you, and then give us effective protection, and increase our happiness, remove the cause of our grief, and save us from sin and memory.

This sacrificial butter is like a precious gem, dear to you. Come near unto this, we pray you, kind fathers: give a gracious hearing to your praises; speak well of us, and confer blessings upon us.

Sitting at your ease at my right hand, may all of you accept these oblations we offer unto you. If we commit any offence against you through our human infirmities, fathers, forgive us.

---

60.   x. 15.

I am but a weak and mortal man, but I give unto you this clarified butter,—it is all I possess. Sitting near these bright flames I have kindled for you, give unto us and to our children enough to live upon—enough to make us happy.

O! Ye bright and omniscient flames, you know all about my fathers, whoever and wherever they all may be. These who are here and those who are not here, those whom we know and those whom we do not know—all, all of them are known to you. Preside at this sacrifice, and accept the food I offer unto you.

The spirit which prompted this hymn determines, indeed, the Hindu attitude towards the dead and has been expressed thus: 'Love and devotion bear no analysis as to their nature, and spurn at the hard realities which would dissolve the charm. We long to show to the spirits of our ancestors that they live in our memory; we realise their embodied existence by the mind's eye, and forgetful of the surrounding world, we become conscious for a moment of their actual presence, and in the exuberance of our feelings we offer them food and water to allay their hunger and thirst.'[61] From this mental condition it is a transition, as soft as it is quick, to the other condition in which the actual presence of the deceased is sought to be counterfeited by the setting up of some symbol such as a stone to represent the body of the deceased.

In the funeral ceremonies of the Brahmanas of south India there obtains a practice, recognised by the authoritative writers, of a small piece of stone being set up immediately after the cremation, in a tiny bower-like enclosure fashioned out of the leaves of the coconut tree, and *pinda* or food is

---

61. Rajkumar-Sarvadhikari, *Hindu Law of Inheritance*, 2nd ed., 158.

 South Indian Portraits in Stone and Metal

offered daily to the stone till the tenth day, when offerings having been made by the agnates also, the stone is removed and consigned to a river or pond in the neighbourhood. By the tenth day, the *preta sarira* seems to be full-fledged and, thereafter, it continues in existence till the *sa-pindi-karana* is performed at the end of a year and the deceased is enrolled among the *pitris*. Even if the south Indian practice has no parallel elsewhere in India, it is by no means opposed to the fundamental notions of the Brahmanical faith as known in the earliest days. Considering that the exigencies of a work-a-day world have greatly curtailed the funeral ceremonies observed in Vedic times (and immediately afterwards),— as where the *sa-pindi-karana* is now performed on the twelfth day instead of on the expiry of twelve months from the death,— we may take it that the south Indian practice preserves the original observances in a very much abbreviated form, the ancient custom having been perhaps to set up a stone in the image of the deceased or to replace the piece of stone on the tenth day by a stone carved into the likeness of the deceased or by a fully worked statue. This would tally, almost closely, with the observances in the Tamil country in respect of the setting up of hero-stones. Ceremonials such as the installing of the memorial-stones in bowers and the offering of food to them show how closely the Vedic and the early Tamil funeral rituals agree. There are a few differences such as that the stone of the Brahmanical ceremonials is not anointed with honey· nor inscribed with the name and the credentials of the hero. The hero-stone being intended for a permanent memorial is appropriately garnished with an inscription, while the stone in the Brahmanical ceremonies receives no such attention.

The difference is susceptible of easy explanation. The hero-stone is a real memorial intended for posterity, while the ceremonial stone of the Brahman funerals represents only the *preta sarira* (corporeal body) of the deceased till the *sa-pindi-karana*— whether performed on the twelfth day or at the end of the twelfth month. With the performance of *sa-pindi-karana* the need for the symbol is past, the deceased having become a *pitri* and, therefore, there is no need to retain the symbol thereafter,— that is, the stone or the statue. Hence it is, perhaps, that no Brahmanical memorial stones or statues have been preserved. Neither Brahmanical texts nor practices could, in their nature, have been opposed to the raising of stones as permanent memorials where permanency was a desideratum, as in the case of memorials to a great warrior or a powerful king. Perhaps such memorial stones evolved gradually into statues, just as the inscribed hero-stones mentioned in the Tamil classics came eventually to be figured as well.

Evidently the *penchant* for symbolisation did not stop short of figuring in stone the features of the deceased person. His *pitris*, the three immediate ancestors, were also represented in statues and ranged in order before his statue so that the process by which he became a *pitri* might be concretely illustrated. The statue of Dasaratha in the *Pratima Nataka* was in all probability installed when Dasaratha was dead but had not yet graduated into a *pitri*. Till the *sa-pindi-karana* ceremony by which he was elevated to that rank, his statue must have stood last in a row of four of which the first three represented his *pitris*. We may perhaps imagine that after *sa-pindi-karana* the *devakula* would contain only the latest three *pitris*, the fourth niche being left

                    South Indian Portraits in Stone and Metal

vacant till death took to it a new tenant on probation for *pitri-ship.* This must be the explanation of why in some *devakulas* three statues are found and why in none have more than four been discovered.

Statues to the living were allowed for what may compendiously be called commemorative and devotional purposes,— such as the images carved in memory of the builder of a temple or in the attitude of holding a burning lamp or plying a fly-whisk,— but were probably forbidden as objects of worship. Such statues, however, became eligible for worship when the subjects whom they represented passed out of this life. All the more so were those statues which were installed as memorials after the subjects' death eligible for being worshipped. In other words, commemorative and devotional statues could evidently be installed even in the lifetime of the subjects but could not be worshipped till their death: memorial stones, however, could be set up on the death of the subjects and be worshipped. When Bhasa enunciates the dictum, by the mouth of one of his characters, that it was not usual for statues to be set up to persons who were alive he must have intended to refer to statues destined for *devakulas.* The hint that a Brahman ought not to worship the images of Kshatriyas seems at first sight to militate against the theory that the worship of sculptural portraits had its origin in the belief that a dead man became a *deva,* but the explanation is to be found in the fact that a *pitri-deva* is not God, but only a *deva* unto his descendants. The wayfarer is admonished to pay his salutations to a hero-stone not because it stands for either the wayfarer's *pitri-deva* or his god, but because it stands for one who had attained *vira-svarga* and, therefore, deserved to be shown honour.

The absence of all vestiges in India of the practice found in Java must be due to the special character of the Hindu belief of a person becoming a *deva* or a god on his death. It is true that the belief is as much a part of the vulgar faith of the Hindu as of his accepted theology, and also of his reasoned philosophy, but the deceased is taken to become a *deva* to his descendants alone and not to the public in general. No Hindu worships another's ancestor as a *deva*, though he would show him the respect due to his exalted position as a *deva*. The distinction between a *deva* and God in Hindu faith and thought is too plain to be mistaken. If, on the one hand, the individuality of the *deva* which is a marked feature of Hindu belief could have led to the image of the *deva* being invested with the features of the deceased— as in the case of the statues of Bhasa,—the fact of the *deva* being such to those alone who were related to him on the earthly side of his existence would have prevented him from graduating into a deity whom all could and must worship. It is hard to decide if the memorial temples were places of general worship. The anxiety, however, to give even the memorial temples the character of places of general worship must have led the Hindu to reject unhesitatingly any temptation to confound the deity with the *deva*. The memorial temples in south India— except in the case of the shrines to saints and preceptors,— were, in all probability temples erected merely in memory of a deceased person, perhaps occasionally on the spot where he died or near the place where he was buried, but they were not tombs raised over the bones or the ashes of the deceased and dedicated to the worship of the person whose remains lay at rest underneath.

     South Indian Portraits in Stone and Metal

The worship offered to statues set up to the deceased is not such worship as is offered to God. It may be that in the case of the saints and the preceptors the ritual of worship is almost as complicated and quite as full of pomp and circumstance as in the ritual of the worship of God, but the pomp and the ceremony are due only to the boundless devotion which the devotee bears to his spiritual masters. In the case of lay persons to whom statues were raised, the worship offered to them must have been only in their character as *devas* and only on behalf of those to whom they were *devas.*

A devotee till death, and a *deva* after it,— this was perhaps the course of the evolution. If in the Brihad isvara temple of Rajaraja I at Tanjore the priest offered worship to the *linga,*— the principal idol,— and also to the statue of Rajaraja, it must be taken that the worship was offered to the *linga* as to God while the worship paid to the image of Rajaraja was merely made by the priest engaged by the Chola kings to their deceased ancestor who had become a *deva* to them.[62] The provision for offerings is only the parallel to the foundations for the saying of mass in Catholic countries.

The group of a *linga* and a statue of a lady, at Kumbhakonam, said to represent Govinda Dikshita and his wife, serves to illustrate a few of the principles underlying the practice of installing images as memorials,— though it would be a great mistake to assume that these principles were accepted by any but those of the sect to which Govinda Dikshita belonged.

---

62. So too in the case of the worship offered to the statues of the Rajputana *devagadhs* or the image of SembiyanMahadevi. The Sakadvipti Brahmanas might partake of the food offered to the statues in the *devagadhs,* because of their poverty or because of customs peculiar to their community.

The *linga*, which is said to be a representation of Govinda Dikshita, cannot in the nature of things be considered a portrait or image of him. The *linga* could have been set up only after the death of Govinda Dikshita. The image of his wife, however, shows her wearing the *mangalya-sutra*, a proof of her husband being alive. We cannot assume that her image came to be set up in the temple during the lifetime of her husband when an image of him had not been also installed, unless we are to make the assumption, for which we have no justification, that she was responsible for the renovation of portions of the temple,— a pious service popularly associated with the name of her husband. Perhaps Govinda Dikshita died before he could complete the renovations and perhaps his wife carried the pious task through, and, in consequence, he was figured in a *linga*, and she in a statue. Though Govinda Dikshita was then dead and his wife could in consequence be portrayed only as a widow, yet the sculptor must have remembered that Govinda Dikshita had become a *linga* and become immortal and that, therefore his wife, though only a relict on this side of the 'Great Divide,' must remain a wife, and so he carves her wearing still the *mangalya-sutra*. The person who was dead being figured in a *linga* and the person who was alive being represented in a statue this group stands in negation of any suggestion that a practice might have obtained in south India of setting up an image in the likeness of a deceased person. Nor were the images installed over the bones or the ashes of Govinda Dikshita or his wife; they are not known to be buried in or near the temple. Moreover, their piety, character and services to the temple qualified them for marks of signal religious honour; and, appropriately, their effigies are placed in a row with the idols of the great saints of Saivism.

IX

CONCLUSION

The varied motives which have inspired the men and women of south India to set up statues and the many forms which these sculptures have taken lead us to doubt whether the art of portrait sculpture can ultimately be traced to one elemental idea.

Occasionally, it has been felt that evil might result from the portraying a person in a statue,— especially if it happened to be very good or very bad,— but the apprehensions have by no means affected the popularity of the art of portraiture.

Statues intended solely to be decorative are almost unknown, but when the sculptor plied his chisel so well as to produce so excellent a relief as Narasimhavarman's or when he fashioned so beautiful a statue as that of Venkata-raya, or when he set up a number of huge statues in a grand Valhalla as at Madura, the sculptor cannot be accused of having lost sight of the decorative value of his productions. A statue such as the one set up to Sita at a sacrifice offered by Rama is merely representative,— its object being to take the place of a person absent in the flesh. Some statues are purely commemorative, like the relievos at Nanaghat which were sculptured as a reminder of the performance of grand sacrifices. Vedanta-Desika made his own statue for exhibiting the many-sideness of his attainments. A large number of the statues are frankly devotional: their main purpose is to exhibit the subjects of sculpture in postures of perpetual service or adoration. Those to which, no worship is offered have been set up for various reasons which range from pride to devotion. Some are votive, accompanying as they do gifts made to gods and godlings. Little medallions or panels carved at the base of statues of gods, Buddhas and saints show the donors venerating the statues carved above them: these devotees merely carry on a tradition which, on Indian soil, is at least as old as the earliest ruins of Mohenjadaro. Indeed, the decorative purpose is evident in every specimen we have come across, except perhaps the *hiranya purusha* of the Vedic sacrifice, and it realises itself as much in crude sketches on stone as in stalwart figures ranged in the huge halls of the great temples.

Many statues are for worship, as where the followers of a particular faith instil portraits of the saints and the preceptors of their persuasion. Sculptured memorials are raised to those who lost their lives in battle or gave up their lives deliberately and they are generally worshipped, but they are rarely portrait statues. Temples are built in memory of kings and queens and others at or adjacent to the spots where they were cremated, but it is highly improbable that they were raised as sepulchres over their corpses or even their ashes. Even if a temple is designed as a memorial, the idol placed in the *sanctum* is a *linga*, and worship is offered to the *linga* as God and not to the deceased. Only when

　　　　　　　South Indian Portraits in Stone and Metal

the sepulchre is that of a religious teacher do we have a statue of him set up over the grave and worship offered to it, but, even then, he is worshipped as himself and not as God. Statues are occasionally installed in memory of men who were dead and were being, or had already been, turned into *devas*, but they were worshipped only by those to whom they were ancestors. If a person pays homage to the sculptural representation of one who was not his ancestor or preceptor, he is to be deemed to offer worship, not to his god or to his preceptor or to a *pitri*, but to have merely shown respect to one who was entitled to receive it on account of his having passed out of the land of the living and become free from the littleness's to which flesh and blood subject us.

A statue to a lay person becomes the object of worship on his death, but even then, the worship is offered only by or on behalf of his descendants. The fundamental notion underlying such worship is that the deceased becomes a *deva* on his death, though only to his descendants, and that as a *deva* he is entitled to honour and respect, though not to worship, from all classes and conditions of men.

The fundamental principles of this cult might have become mixed up with the notions pertaining to cults such as those of the menhir and the hero, and till more material is available it is not possible to arrive at a just estimate of the extent to which the various notions have influenced one another.

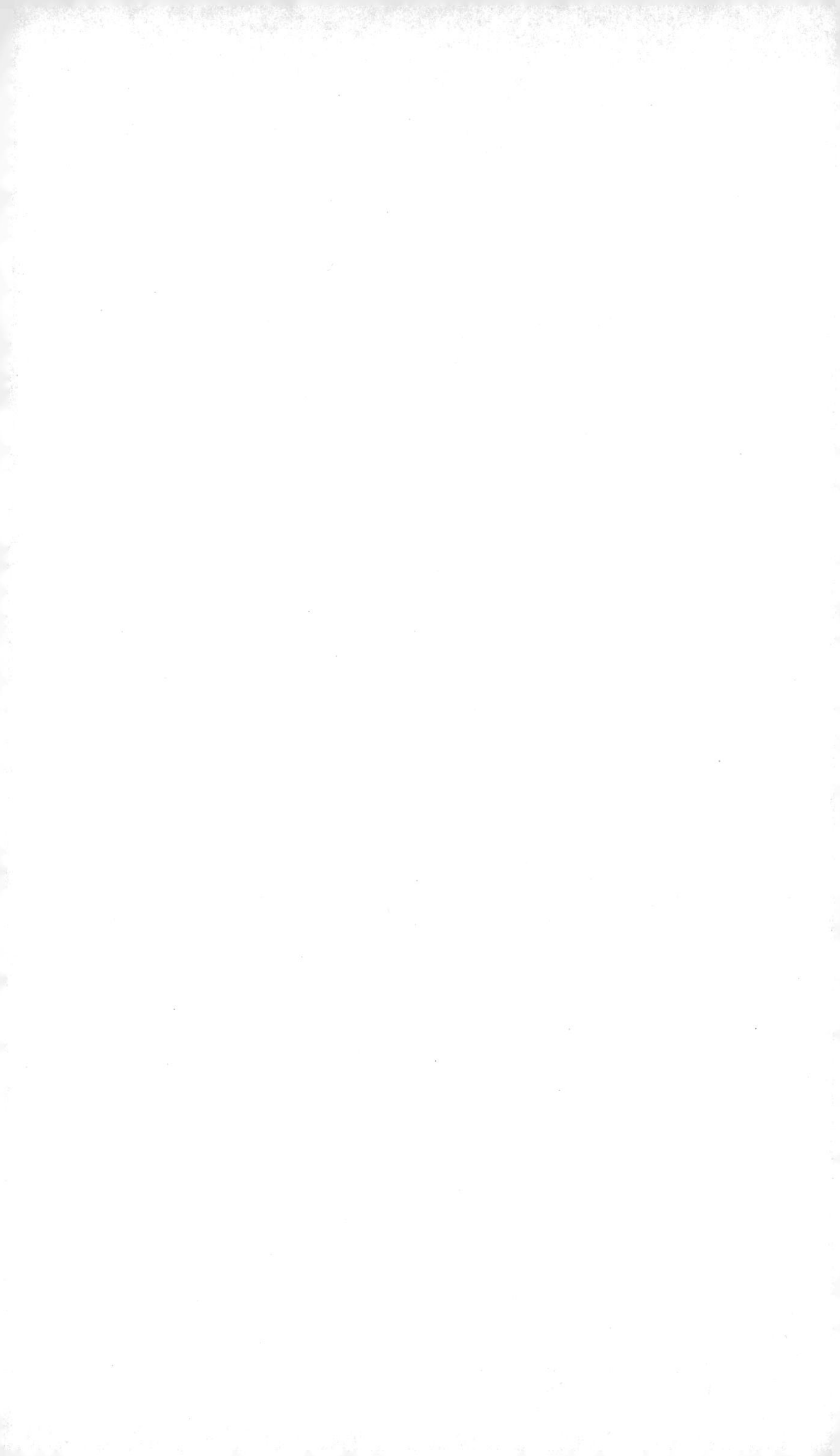

9 789390 697496